International trademark design a handbook of marks of identity by Peter Wildbur

International trademark design a handbook of marks of identity by Peter Wildbur

Barrie & Jenkins
Communica-Europa

I would like to thank the designers and
owners of trademarks who have contributed
material and information for this book.

I am also indebted to Colin Cohen for a very
helpful discussion about the technicalities
of watermarks.

My special thanks to John Blandford for the
production artwork for this volume.

First published in 1979 by
Barrie and Jenkins Ltd
24 Highbury Crescent, London N5 1RX

© Peter Wildbur 1979

ISBN 0 214 20309 7

6   Introduction

7   **Communication and graphic signs**

19   **Marks of identity**

25   **Some practical aspects of designing a trademark**

33   **Some early forms of trademarks**

47   **A collection of international trademark designs:**

section 1   49   Resources
2   53   The environment
3   61   Transportation
4   67   Industry
5   75   Products
6   83   The high street
7   89   Services
8   99   Communications
9 105   Entertainment & sport
10 113   Organisations & societies

123   **Registering a trademark**

128   Book list and trademark organisations

129   Index of designers

132   Index of clients

Acknowledgements

The photographs of Dutch road signs on pages 8-9 courtesy Dr Herbert Spencer.

Illustrations on pages 12-13 reproduced by permission from a series of articles by Heinrich Fleischacker in *TM Magazine,* St Gallen, Switzerland.

Photograph on page 17 by courtesy of *Design,* Colin Curwood.

The line illustrations on pages 34-35 are reproduced by permission from *Art of the Watermark* by Walter Herdeg, The Graphis Press, Zurich, Switzerland.
The beta-radiograph photographs courtesy of the Bodleian Library, Oxford.

Illustrations on pages 36-39 reproduced by permission from *English Merchants' Marks* by F. A. Girling, The Lion and Unicorn Press, London.

Illustrations of firemarks on pages 40-41 from the Bashall Dawson Collection, courtesy of The Chartered Insurance Institute, London. Photographs by Richard Bryant.

Illustrations on pages 44-46 are from 'London Tradesmen's Cards of the XVIII century' courtesy of B T Batsford Ltd.

Introduction

The word 'trademarks' can be misleading by giving the impression that it is only related to the products of trade and manufacturing industry. Trademarks were certainly used for this purpose in their earliest forms as merchant marks, watermarks and hallmarks and this continued to be their chief use following the great increase in the number of machine made products after the industrial revolution. Gradually the scope of the trademark widened, despite the lack of legal protection for marks other than those applied to products. Trademarks used today are almost unlimited in their scope and perhaps the term 'mark of identity' would be more appropriate to cover the activities of such diverse organisations as airlines, banks, sporting bodies, local authorities and political pressure groups.
This change in emphasis from a product or brand mark to a mark of identity for an organisation has been a slow one but one that looks as if it will continue and there are indications that the legal protection afforded to product marks will soon be extended to cover companies which provide services, skills or information. A more recent development has been the growing use of the certification mark which is a registered mark shared by any number of groups with a common interest in standards.

There used to be a party game which consisted of seeing how many well known trademarks the player could identify. For most city dwellers today the number of marks that any adult can put a name to must run into the hundreds with many more that can be generally recognised. This is of some interest since trademarks are not images that we have to memorise for reasons of practical use, such as airport signs, or for reasons of safety, such as road or factory signs. Unfortunately our memory of a trademark, however banal the mark may be is quite often based on the frequency of our exposure to it but one of the aims of this book is to suggest that a well designed and well researched mark is likely to be more memorable to a wide audience and therefore more effective than a poorly designed or off-the-shelf variety.

In most fields of graphic communication the object is to convey a message with the minimum of ambiguity. In the case of trademark design this is seldom the case and in fact alternative meanings can, and often are, deliberately built into a design. To this extent the trademark allows for an interpretation of meaning and this ambiguity of idea expressed through precise linear forms is one of the distinguishing features of a trademark design.

This book is divided into sections which can be seen as different facets of the subject. The main part of the book is a collection of trademarks showing the work of both established and little known designers.

Communication and graphic signs

Human beings communicate with each other mainly through the medium of signs. I am using the word 'sign' to mean the written or printed image rather than through physical gestures of body language although both are equally valid forms of communication. In primitive societies signs are often based on pictorial images which directly, or by association, express some quality of the original. Such systems are limited in expressive range and require a large number of sign elements even to provide a very basic language for everyday communication and for storing information.

The evolution of these pictographic systems into our present highly flexible alphabets is well documented but it would be useful to point out that the main characteristic of alphabetic systems is that they operate at a linear level with letters, sounds and words being put together in a strict order. The direction of 'reading' may be horizontal or vertical but the sequence remains fixed unlike graphic signs which can be designed to operate in one or more directions.

The letters of the alphabet are only one type of graphic sign and what I would like to do in this chapter is to describe some of the other types of signs and to put them together into a sign 'spectrum'. From this we shall be able to see which areas are the most effective from a trademark point of view and it may enable us to diagnose why certain graphic elements in a design are incompatible with others. The designer in producing a trademark is usually working to a time limitation and therefore some analytical knowledge of the types of sign available to him can be as useful as colour theory in avoiding some of the pitfalls in combining colours.

In describing signs we come up against the difficulty of finding suitably descriptive term since most existing words in everyday use, such as symbol, emblem, logotype have a very wide meaning and are often used inter-changeably even amongst designers. On the other hand I would wish to avoid the highly technical terms used by some writers on communication theory, many of whom, I suspect, create their own vocabularies. I have based the following categories on Maldonado's glossary of graphic signs ('Glossary of Semiotics' by Tomas Maldonado, *Uppercase 5,* Whitefriars Press, London 1961), which provides a good basic definition and which has the advantage of being applicable to other fields of communication.

In describing types of signs we can first make a simple distinction between signs which represent or stand for sounds (phonograms) and those which are non-phonetic in origin (logograms).

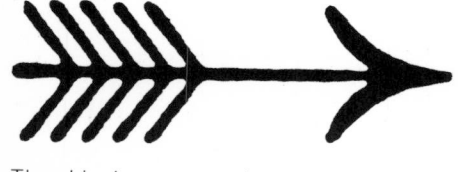

The ubiquitous arrow sign was probably first used during the early 19th century.
Its stylised form is now universally accepted as a vehicle direction sign.

Dutch road sign

Phonogram		**Logogram**		
Phonetic sign		Abstract sign		Representational sign (pictogram)

Figure 1

Phonogram		**Logogram**		
Phonetic sign	Phonetic/abstract sign	Abstract sign	Symbolic sign	Representational sign (pictogram)

Figure 2

Phonogram		**Logogram**		
Phonetic sign	Phonetic/abstract sign	Abstract sign	Symbolic sign	Representational sign (pictogram)
A phonetic visual language sign coded to certain sounds. Prosodic signs are used to represent properties of speech such as length, accent and pause	Combining phonetic and abstract elements	Non-phonetic and non-representational	Makes use of one or more representational forms to convey a complex or abstract idea	Based on pictorial referents usually without any secondary meaning

Figure 3

Dutch road sign

Signpost, Westerham, Kent

Logograms can be divided into two distinct types: those based on non-pictorial sources (abstract) and those based on pictorial referents (representational). See figure 1, page 9.

Between these three broad groups we can introduce two more categories which share some of the characteristics of those on either side of them. See figure 2, page 9.

Within these five groups we can place most forms of graphic sign ranging from a character of an alphabet to an internationally understood road sign. Before going on to describe these types of sign in more detail we can summarise them as shown in figure 3, page 9.

These sign groups, like colours in the spectrum, have no firm dividing lines but the ability to distinguish essential differences between signs will help us both as designers and users of marks.

It is not, of course, the only way of classifying signs which range from attempts to classify by shape and pattern for documentation and registration purposes to classification by product or service.

Trademarks can fall into one or more of these categories but the majority lie within the middle three sections. The first section includes all marks consisting mainly of letters or words, including invented words, and the last section includes signs and sign systems where the pictorial representation stands for a simple, often single, item of information.

1
Canadian National Railways
Designer / Allan Flemming, Canada
Art Director / James Valkus

Phonetic sign

his is a visual language sign representing a
ertain sound. The basic signs are the letters
f the alphabet but while, in the English
anguage, we accept that there are twenty
ix characters we should feel ourselves
onsiderably deprived if we were unable to
se the much larger range of characters in
eneral use. As children we have to learn to
ecognise 26 capital letters and about 18
ower case letters (the c o p s v w x z are
ufficiently close to their capital form)
ogether with an ampersand (&) 10 numerals
nd a set of prosodic signs (; : , . ' ' ? !)

anguage has evolved over a long period of
me and changes in the spoken form have
ed to modifications of certain letters and the
ddition of new ones. Today there are
ressures to reform the English language, to
ationalise its spelling and pronounciation
nd these could lead to further changes in
ur alphabet. (See 'The Sound-Spell, an
lphabet and a policy' and 'Soundspel — an
merican approach to a phonetic alphabet',
cographic no. 9, International Council of
raphic Design Associations, 1976).

Roman alphabet

Digital letters

Computer alphabet

2

rtone
esigners/Seymour Chwast and Milton
laser, USA

3
The Plessey Company Ltd
Designer/Norbert Dutton FSIA,UK

4
Equal Opportunities Commission
(Government Agency)
Designer/Kenneth Hollick FSIAD,UK

Apart from the large number of basic characters, our alphabet is available in a very large range of type faces or letterforms which are being added to almost daily. Many of these are of ephemeral character but some interpretations of letters for machine reading and electronic printouts are important from the way we have to modify our reading habits and may influence new alphabets in the future.

One of the characteristics of the phonetic sign is that it is a 'coded' language, that is to say that it can be transposed from one sign system into another, from the printed character to braille, the morse code or semaphore.

Deaf and dumb alphabet

Semaphore alphabet

International signal flags

Braille alphabet

Morse code

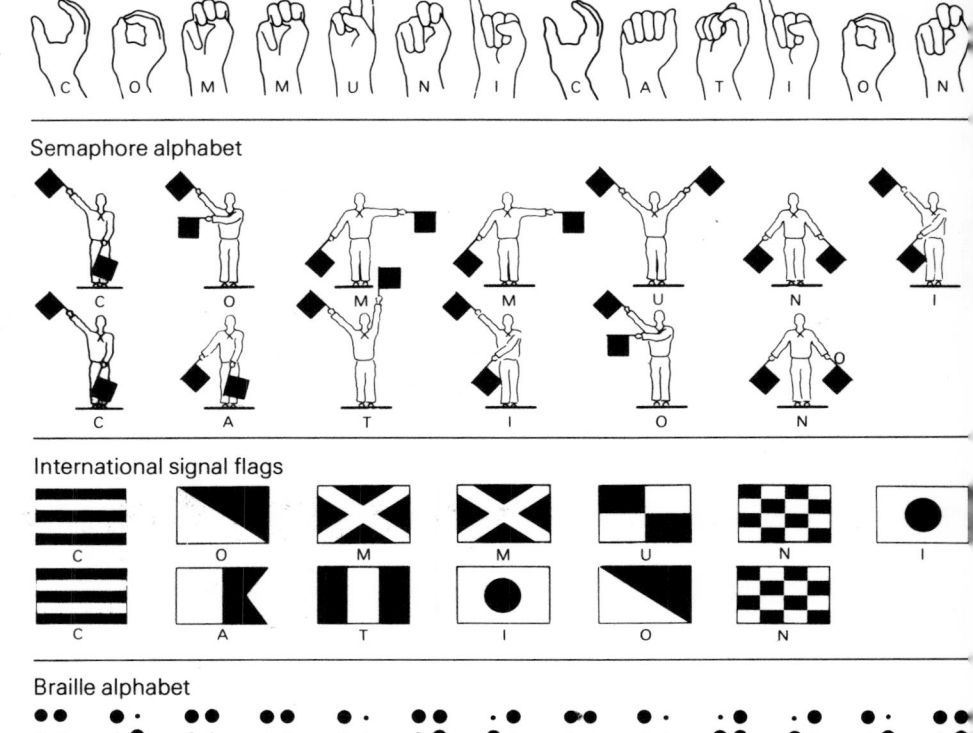

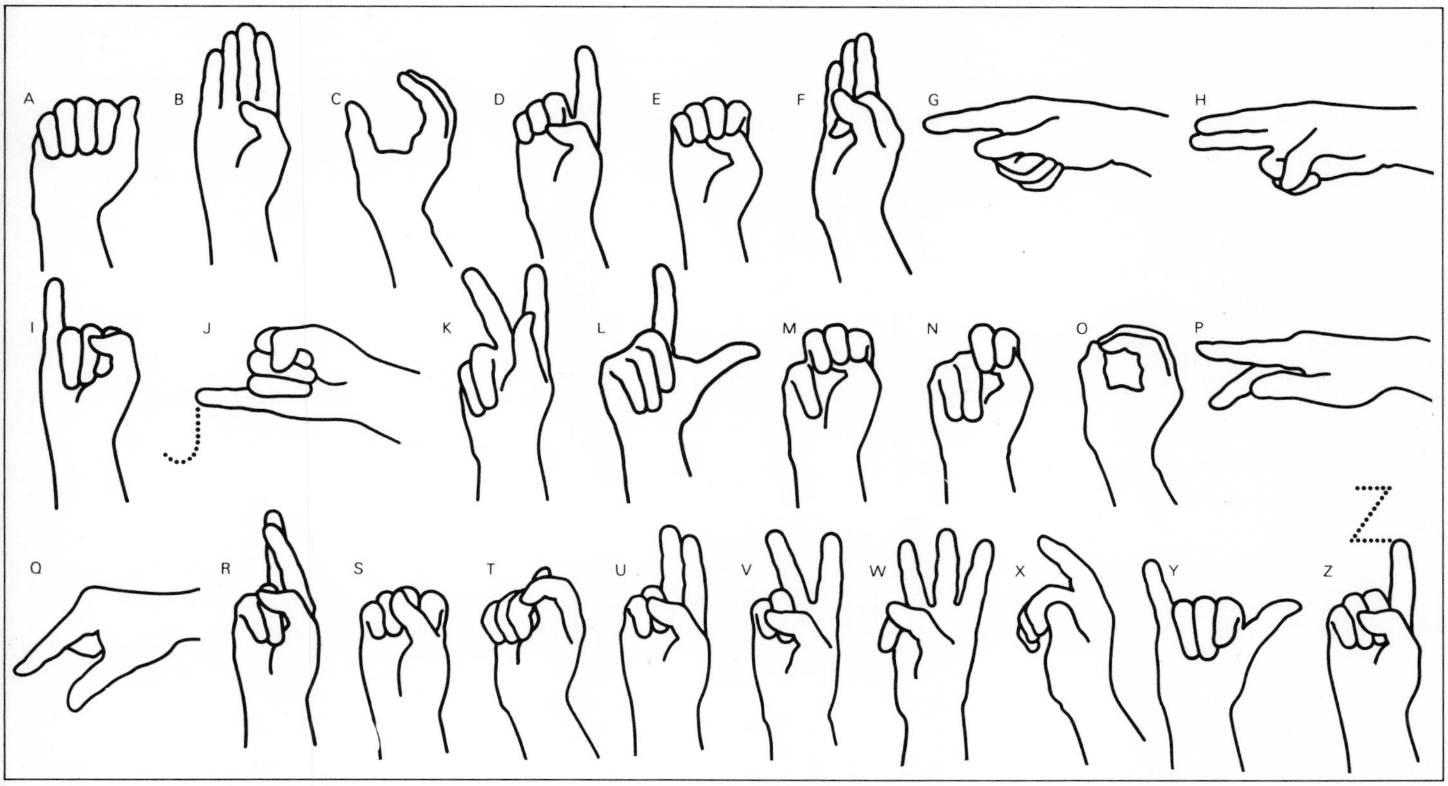

A B C D E F G H

I J K L M N O P

Q R S T U V W X Y Z

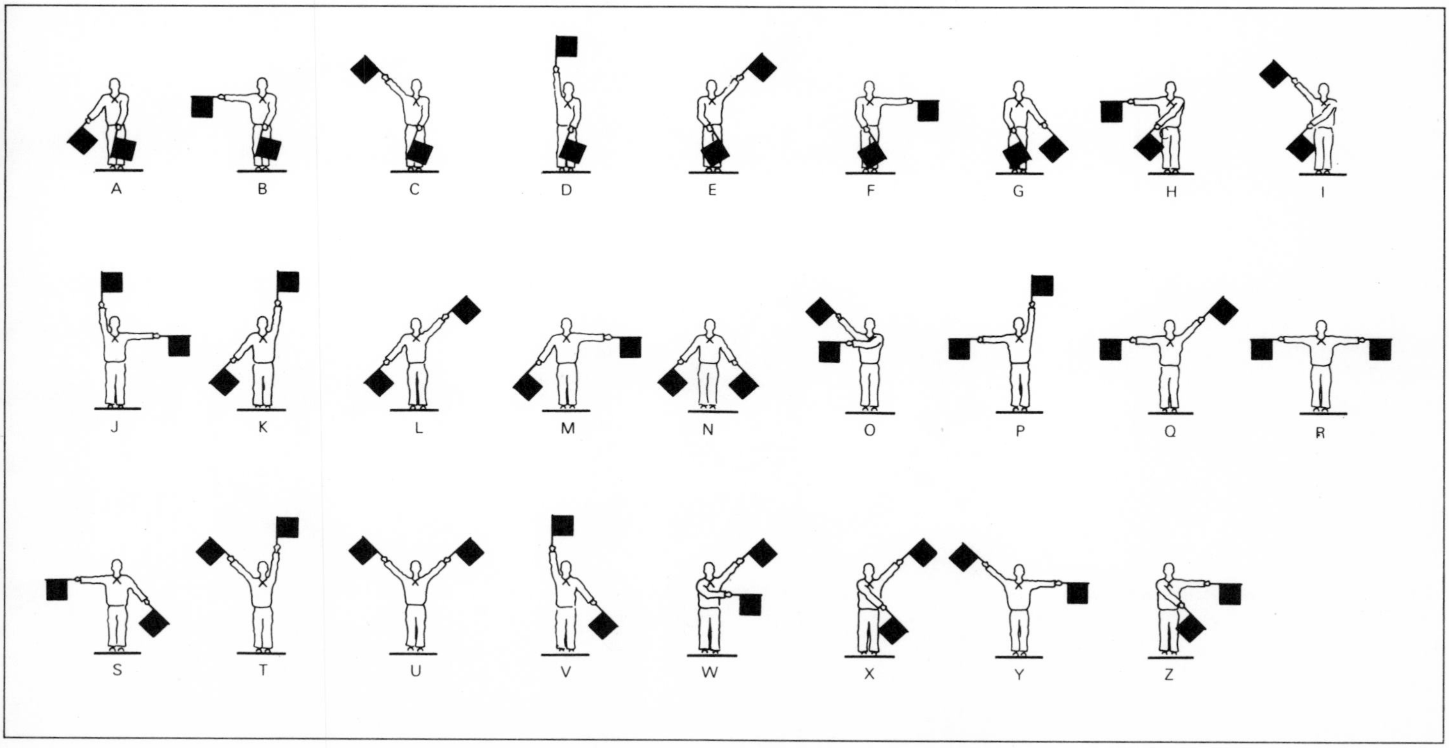

A B C D E F G H I

J K L M N O P Q R

S T U V W X Y Z

Phonetic/abstract sign

This type of sign combines words or letters with abstract forms. In some cases the abstract elements merely emphasise the character or meaning of a word while in others the letter forms are treated as abstract elements and are used for their shape and pattern values to the exclusion of their original phonetic meaning.

The photograph below shows a boat timetable in which the stencilled phonetic characters are beginning to merge into an abstract pattern.

Further examples of this type of design can be found in the marks for the Alireza Group of Companies, 1/1 on page 49 and Trissl Lift, 9/28 on page 111.

Boat excursion sign

5
Swiss Gymnastic Association
Designer/Peter Kräuchi ASG,SWB, Switzerland
Mark based on the four F's of the Association

6
Quebec Hydro-Electric
Designer/Gagnon, Valkus Inc, Canada

7
Deutsches Fernsehen
(Competition for German Television)
Designer/Anton Stankowski, West Germany

Abstract sign

This is a non-representational type of sign although the design may be derived from a representational image through deliberate simplification or stylisation. Even in the most abstract designs it is possible to 'read' representational meanings into the design and this can be deliberately invoked by the designer.

A good example of this type of design is a mark for Compagnie Financière et du Crédit SA, 7/3 on page 90.

This type of sign has usually to be learnt as its meaning will not be immediately obvious and so it is important that the design be as different as possible from any competing designs. This quality of uniqueness is difficult to achieve in practice owing to the vast number of designs now in circulation and the limited number of primary shapes from which the designer can select.

No entrance road sign

Austrian national flag

8
Herman Miller Inc
Designer/Irving Harper, George Nelson & Co Inc, USA

9
The International Olympic Committee symbol
Designer/Pierre de Coubertin

The official colours for the symbol are blue, yellow, black, green and red

10
Shinko Electric Company Ltd
Designer/Kenichi Yoshioka, Japan

11
Irish Double Jersey Association
Designer/Patrick Scott, Irish Republic

Symbolic sign

A combination of abstract and representational elements enables this type of sign to have an immediate recognition value. Its particular characteristic is to go beyond the limited meaning of a purely representational sign and by the juxtaposition of images convey a wider meaning using similar principles to montage.

In some cases it is possible to use methods of optical illusion to get the negative as well as the positive shapes in a design to convey an image only one of which can be seen at any one time. This can have the effect of a 'subliminal' image.

Examples of symbolic signs are the marks for the National Theatre (project), 9/1 on page 105 and the Black Sea Music Festival, 9/10 on page 108.

Representational sign (pictogram)

This is an image related sign which represents, or stands for, the object depicted. It may stand for the single object or for all types of that object as for instance in a pictogram of an aircraft at an airport. Its most successful use is where it stands directly for an object rather than for some property of that object or the result of interaction with that object. If we take three simple pictograms we can see how effective they are in these contexts: first a pictogram of a telephone; this has a direct unambiguous relation to the object. Secondly, a pictogram of a wine glass which may mean wine glass or drinking, but may be used to stand for an abstract concept such as 'fragile' or even 'this way up'. The third example is a pictogram of a skull which is commonly used to denote 'poison' or even 'danger'. The degree of interpretation possible varies considerably and this must be borne in mind when a pictogram is selected.

A pictogram is difficult to recognise if the object is not fairly well known by its shape or has a poorly defined shape. For instance, a motor horn is a commonplace object but not, in present day examples, one that many people would easily recognise in pictographic form.

Pictograms if they portray a man-made object, are likely to date very rapidly and will need constant redrawing to keep them up to date. This is particularly true of objects

12
Cliche-Schwitter AG
(Process engravers)
Designer/Gerstner, Gredinger + Kutter,
Switzerland

13
**Büro für Werbung, Organisation und
Sozialprobleme**
(Social services)
Designer/Eugen and Max Lenz, Switzerland

14
The Law Society
(Mark for Legal Aid Scheme)
Designer/Richard Daynes FSIAD, London

which are subject to rapid technological change such as aircraft and vehicles. It seems to be true that as man-made objects become more complex the outer shape of the object becomes less characteristic of that particular item and less easy to differentiate as a graphic image.

A further limitation of a pictogram is that people from different cultures, even within the same country, may not recognise or give the same interpretation to a pictogram.

A pictogram, therefore, requires care in selection both to the time scale involved and the context of its use.

Bicycle track pictogram

15
Olympic Games, Munich
Designer/Otl Aicher, West Germany

Pictograms for track and field events, swimming and football

16
United States Department of Transportation
Designers/Cook and Shanosky
Associates Inc, Princeton, New Jersey

These graphic symbols (part of a set of 33 symbols) have been produced by the American Institute of Graphic Arts (AIGA). To develop this system of transportation symbols an 'inventory' of symbols was collected from 24 different sources from all over the world. These were then analysed for effectiveness by a design committee which made recommendations on the final concept for each new symbol.

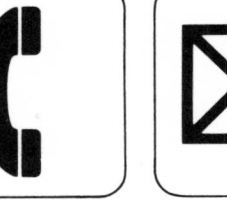

Marks of identity

Creating a design for a trademark presents a challenge to most designers for not only has the designer to reconcile the demands of the client's brief which may be very specific in its requirements but he has to ensure that the final design is capable of reduction to postage stamp size, or smaller, without loss of character or definition. The design, in most cases, must be capable of working in black and white since it is almost inevitable that the mark will be reproduced at some time in newspapers or on black and white tv.

The more demanding requirements of a trademark are those of uniqueness, at least within the client's field of activity and some degree of timelessness. The latter is a quality which can best be ensured in a negative way by not using fashionable visual cliches or type faces which are likely to become dated in a few years. One cannot hope to escape some 'period' quality other than by using basic geometrical forms but Walter Herdeg has summed up this requirement perfectly when he says, 'A firm and its registered trademark may well be old, for age shows that they have stood the test of time; but a trademark that is out-of-date is, in both senses of the word, a bad sign!'

There are, of course, occasions when an element of fashion may be particularly important in a design such as a mark for a fashion designer, a night club or a magazine but the projected time span of the mark will usually dictate the type of solution. Many old trademark designs in this country have been deliberately retained because the period element in the design is of very real value in stressing their traditional virtues. In some cases the original designs remain unaltered but in others they have been carefully simplified for reproduction in small sizes and on different materials.

Amongst the more practical contraints affecting the final design are those of the media and reproduction process. It is quite common for a trademark specification to call for its use in embossed, stencilled, woven or illuminated versions apart from the conventional reproduction processes. For many of these special uses the design can be easily adapted but a major application for a particular medium will have to take into account the prevailing limitations or technology of the medium itself. The use of neon tubes before fluorescent, back-lit signs became widespread is an example where a linear emphasis was derived from the medium in much the same way as in early forms of watermarks (see page 34).

The problem of scale, already touched on, does become important when designs have to be capable of very large as well as very small reproduction. In most cases these will require the preparation of several basic versions of a design in which such things as

he problem of line weight, optical effects,
nk spread or tv screen interference patterns
re taken into account.

he coordination of a mark into a corporate
dentity scheme may require the preparation
f a detailed constructional grid to enable
he design to be reconstructed in parts of the
vorld where photographic reproduction or
nlargement is not available. The geometric
r simplified form of construction required
or this purpose may again influence the
nal form of the mark.

n considering the content of a trademark
esign we can separate three elements
vhich are found in most designs. These are
he descriptive, the symbolic and the
ypographic and they can be found either
ingly or in combination.

Descriptive marks

The inclusion of some *descriptive* visual
image relating to a clients' products is an
obvious element in creating a new mark but
may present a number of problems in such a
small design format. Any one product
reference automatically excludes others and
an attempt to combine several products or
elements common to most of them seldom
produces a satisfactory visual result.
A product itself must also be expected to
change, both internally and externally, over
a period of time and major functional
changes, such as the change from piston to
jet engines in aircraft, can make any design
obsolete that relies on a purely descriptive
image. In many cases there is a change in
the emphasis of a companys' products with
time and some product ranges may
disappear altogether. For these reasons it is
often more important to suggest the
character of an organisation than to show
its products.

7
Cunic Partition Systems
Designer/Romek Marber, London

he mark is based on a section of the basic
tructural component

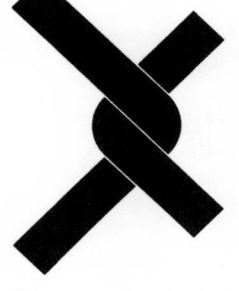

18
Barnards wire fencing
Designer/Romek Marber, London

The mark is based on the basic twisting
feature common to all wire fencing

19
Resilience Ltd
(Manufacturers of springs for bedding and
upholstery)
Designer/Peter Wildbur, London

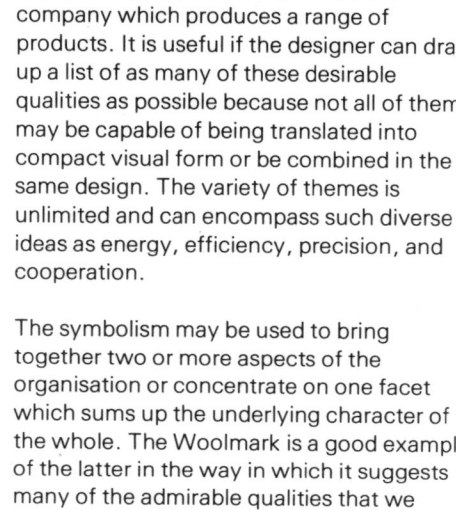

20
Project for an American
pharmaceutical laboratory
Designer/Peter Kräuchi ASG,SWB,
Switzerland

Mark based on the initial letter D

Symbolic marks

With the widespread use of trademarks by organisations who provide services, skills or information the descriptive approach is of little use and one must create an image *symbolising* some abstract quality of the organisation. This symbolic approach may be just as appropriate, however, for a company which produces a range of products. It is useful if the designer can draw up a list of as many of these desirable qualities as possible because not all of them may be capable of being translated into compact visual form or be combined in the same design. The variety of themes is unlimited and can encompass such diverse ideas as energy, efficiency, precision, and cooperation.

The symbolism may be used to bring together two or more aspects of the organisation or concentrate on one facet which sums up the underlying character of the whole. The Woolmark is a good example of the latter in the way in which it suggests many of the admirable qualities that we associate with wool in a single image. The image selected by its designer is instantly recognisable and manages to convey those overtones of meaning by associating the natural raw material with the craft qualities of hand knitting.

There are a number of conventional and popular symbols which every designer files away at the back of his mind and which can best be described as off-the-shelf symbols. These can be of value since the symbolism is firmly established in the viewer's mind and all that is required is an appropriate graphic form. Some typical examples of these are: dove/peace, tortoise/slow, lightning flash/electrical danger, entwined snake/medicine (for a classic example of this symbol see George Staehelin's mark for Pharma Information, 10/30 on page 120.

For symbolising events of a national or international character, the designer can draw on a large field of formal and patriotic emblems including flags and heraldic devices. Heraldry however is an area to view with caution. Originally a vigourous form of personal identification combined with genealogical information it now appears to have become so institutionalised that the formal rules have replaced any concern for visual qualities.

21
International Wool Secretariat
Designer/Francesco Saroglia, Italy

A certification trade mark for products of pure new wool

22
Irish Silk Poplin
Designer/Louis le Brocquy RHA,FSIAD,
D.Litt, France

Mark based on a stylised female silk moth

23
Chicago Pharmacal
Designer/John Massey, USA

4
enneth Harris
Hearing aid consultant)
Designer/Ron Ford FSIAD, Bristol

Typographic marks

A good many trade marks make use of letter forms, sometimes because an existing mark has been registered as a word or initial letters. In some cases the designer uses letter forms as a starting point much as a composer might compose a piece of music around a set of notes. This *typographic* approach requires more than a collection of letters to qualify as a trademark. It has to contain some graphic organisation or addition to its formal content which will enhance or characterise the nature of the client's activity. This may be achieved by the addition of some new element or by distorting or regrouping the letterforms to express qualities of the product as well as retaining to some degree their alphabetic meaning. The letters themselves do not have to be recognisable to produce an effective mark but either result is justified if the designer has been able to arrive at an appropriate and memorable design.

Having selected the most appropriate elements for a mark the design process is one of fusing these statements into a formal whole and synchronising them in such a way that form and meaning become inseparable. There are several examples in this book of designs created by the combination of two simple images, each of which is recognisable on its own but which achieves new meaning by juxtaposition. Stephan Kantscheff demonstrates this in his mark for a music festival held on the Black Sea coast where

he has combined the image of a musical stave with a sea horse in such a way that the negative image of one becomes the positive image of the other, 9/10 on page 108. Contrasting images of flask and flames are combined in Tor Pettersen's mark for Chelsea Drug and Chemical Company, 5/1 on page 75.

A design for a trademark can be of almost any external shape but any collection of marks will show that most designs are of a compact nature so that regardless of use and in whatever type of context they retain their individuality and remain isolated from other graphic features.

A glance through this book will show how limited, in one sense, the trademark designer's vocabulary is with, only rarely, the luxury of an additional colour. A large proportion of these designs are composed with simple geometric shapes bounded by a straight line or compass curve and often utilising lines of equal thickness throughout. With such a limited range of shapes, reminiscent of a composer's keyboard, the designer has to make every detail of the design work for him with the 'negative' shapes, that is the white spaces left between the black 'positive' areas, treated as an additional element in the composition. A good example of this is the mark by Rolf Harder for the Canadian Association for Retarded Children, 10/8 on page 115 and a

25
Kilkenny Design Workshops
Designer/Louis le Brocquy RHA, FSIAD, D.Litt, France

26
Delta Acceptance Corporation Ltd
(Finance company)
Designer/Chris Yaneff, Canada

Mark based directly on the Greek letter

mark for the Central Office of Information designed by June Fraser and Mike Butts, 7/12 on page 92.

From this point of view, the starting point for the designer can equally well be a geometric shape, a letter form or a conventional image.

To some extent, the designer must be able to view his images with the eyes of a child· two horizontally placed dots can equally well stand for eyes as for rollers of a printing press; a heart shape can signify computer dating or, by a shift of emphasis, a cardiac research centre. The designer becomes a magician only needing to indicate the context of the image to set it firmly and unambiguously for us.

The designer learns to manipulate shapes and forms much as a composer learns to build notes but only a few designers achieve that magical quality which can transform merely black and white shapes into a memorable and human image.

27
Certina
(Swiss watchmaker)
Designer/Carl B Graf ASG,SWB,
Switzerland

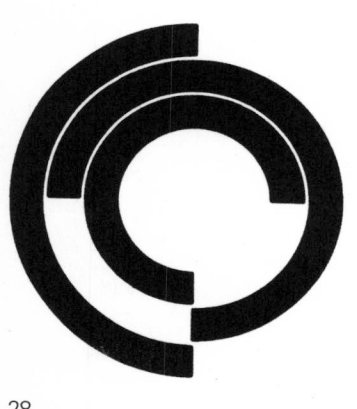

28
Jon G Darby
(Photographer)
Designer/Jonathan de Morgan, Leeds,
England

29
Associated Adhesives Ltd
Designer/Peter Gauld FSIAD, London

30
**Canadian Sociology and Anthropology
Association**
Designer/Burton Kramer, Toronto, Canada

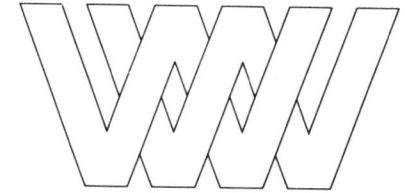

31
Wilson Walton Signs Ltd
Designer/Alan Fletcher, Pentagram, London

Some practical aspects of designing a trademark

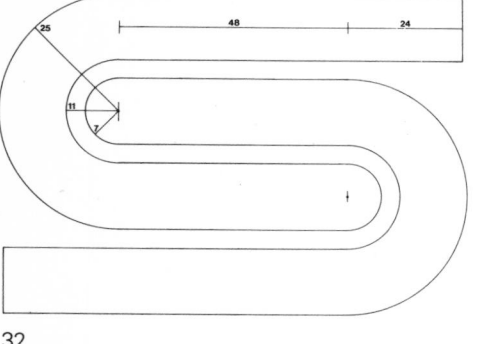

32
Constructional drawing for a trademark for
the British Steel Corporation designed by
David Gentleman. (See 1/14 on page 52 for
complete version of mark)

These notes on the practical aspects of
trademark design are inevitably personal in
nature and describe how the author sets
about designing a new mark.

In most types of designing there is always an
element of 'inspiration' which may enable
the designer to conceive the solution or even
the final form of a mark in a short space of
time. Usually, however, it is a matter of
sheer hard work and the discarding of many
draft designs before a workable and
acceptable solution emerges. In the absence
of such short cuts it is very desirable to have
a working 'pattern' which will enable the
designer to make steady progress towards a
solution of what sometimes seems to be an
impossible problem, and the following notes
are a description of one such 'pattern'.

Briefing

Briefing by a client on the requirements of a
new mark may vary from a single sentence
to a ten page typed document. Somewhere
between these extremes is the optimum
amount of information that the designer
needs to know if he is to produce a mark
which will take account of present and
future uses of the mark. If too little
information is available then the designer
should draw up a list of questions, or a check
list, to enable him to obtain this important
information. A great deal of time can be
wasted if some important element

(sometimes a negative element) is missing
from the first presentation of the design due
to the lack of a proper briefing.

We can list some typical items on such a
check list as follows:

What is the anticipated audience for the
mark (local, national, international,
worldwide)?

Is the design required for a single mark or
will it be used as the basis for a number of
related (divisional) marks?

Will the mark be used with any other existing
marks, take the place of other marks or be
entirely new?

Is the mark to be used on its own or in
relation to a company name, brand name
etc?

Is the mark to incorporate letters or words?

Estimated range of uses in terms of media:
architectural, signing, livery, print, tv etc?

Is the mark to be the basis for a corporate
identity programme?

The answers to such a check list will usually
generate further questions and, in some
cases, cause the client to rethink some part
of the brief.

33 (right)
Constructional drawing by Otl Aicher for the
multi-colour version of the International
Olympic Committee five-ring emblem
showing compensation for the optical
'weight' of each colour

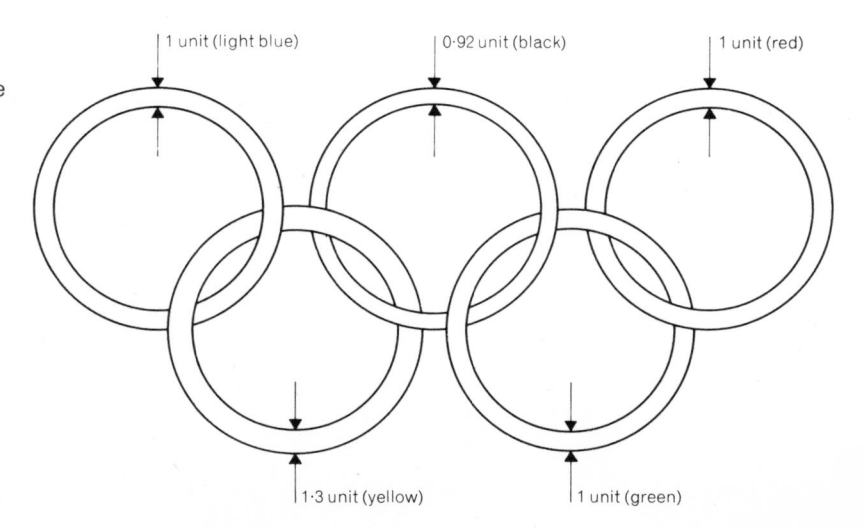

34 (left)
Constructional drawing for the symbol for the Games of the XXI Olympiad, Montreal designed by George Huel, Canada (see 9/22 on page 110 for complete version of symbol). The illustration shows a page from the design manual giving details for constructing the symbol from a grid.

Detail below shows the version for reproduction in small sizes showing optical corrections made between the inter-sections of the circles and vertical strokes.

V 10   V 20   V 30   V 40   V 50   V 60   V 70   V 80   V 90   V 100   V 110   V 120   V 130

35
Constructional drawing for a trademark for Compagnie Financière et du Crédit SA, Switzerland, designed by David Gentleman. (See 7/3 on page 90 for complete version of mark).

From this information, the designer can draw up basic parameters within which to produce his design. He will then know that his design is unlikely to be faulted at a later stage due to the omission of some vital information at the briefing.

I find it best to go through this preliminary stage very thoroughly but then to file the information away at the back of my mind since, in most cases, it will not contribute any positive thinking about the new design. At its best it will enable you to avoid imagery or emphasis which you might otherwise have spent time on researching.

Image selection

Given the nature of the problem, and some of the constraints, the designer can begin to explore and put together the visual elements which will form the raw material of the design. In the case of a difficult problem, such as conveying visually a complex, abstract idea, I find it useful to write down a list of verbal associations with the theme. This list, if put down quickly, may produce a number of unexpected themes — many non-visual, but resulting in images or motifs which may later be combined. The fact that some of these words may be abstract terms can provide other, perhaps more visual, associations. This method of generating visual equivalents for a given item is only one approach and each designer no doubt

formulates his own method of selecting imagery.

In the case of a trademark design for a manufacturer, a visit to the factory will be an important step in acquiring knowledge of the company's products as well as manufacturing processes. Striking images may result from observation of some part of the production sequence or even in the inspection techniques. For one of my own designs for a spring manufacturer I was able to use a particular type of zig-zag spring taken from the production line.

Techniques

Getting down to the more practical problems of working tools, I find that a felt or marker pen is more useful in the drafting stages of a design than a pencil. The pen can be chosen to give any selected line thickness and large areas of solid tone can rapidly be filled in to give an almost exact impression of the mass and line of the evolving design.

By contrast, a pencil, even a soft one, gives a soft line and textured solids. An even more flexible design method is to use a sharp pair of scissors with black and white paper or card. This technique has the advantage that each element can be moved, repositioned, taken away and replaced before the design is 'fixed' by rubber gum or transparent tape. A cutting blade for use in an ordinary drafting

36 (right)
From a range of pictograms designed by Otl Aicher, Alfred Kern and Gerhard Joksch (courtesy of Erco Leuchten GmbH, West Germany). These are all based on the grid at right.

compass (it replaces the pencil lead) is an extremely useful accessory for quickly cutting perfect circles in paper.

No doubt we shall soon be able to project and compose designs on a tv screen which may be the ultimate in flexibility of designing but our present methods do at least enable us to keep a record of the stages in designing and provide a valuable record of the development of an idea through different visual treatments.

As most trademark designs will need to be capable of reduction it is useful to have a reducing glass in your tool kit so that the reduced image size can be checked as the design progresses. These reducing lenses are not easy to find in the shops but the larger lenses taken from old slide projectors or viewers can sometimes be adapted for this purpose. Besides revealing any problems of line thickness and the filling in of white spaces the change of scale can be useful in viewing the design. One of the problems of working on a small scale, monochrome design is that of being able to see it with fresh eyes. Another way of obtaining a new viewpoint of a design is to view the reversed image in a mirror.

One useful point to bear in mind during the preliminary planning of a mark is that designs which have no specific vertical or horizontal reference points can very easily be set at the wrong angle by a contractor or printer. Designs within a circle or multi-sided shape suffer from this problem. The solution is to build into the design at an early stage an element which can be aligned with type matter or a frame (in my mark for the British Gliding Association, 9/25 on page 111, the base of the fuselage elements is intended to be horizontal when positioned correctly).

Grids

Some designers find it helpful to work out a design over a piece of graph paper or a specially constructed grid. The lines of the grid appearing to act as a form of scaffolding for the design. The choice of line thickness, positioning and direction is limited by the simplicity or complexity of the grid and this provides a limited number of choices in producing a design. I personally find this method too limiting unless I am designing a set of images (let us say a set of pictograms for signing purposes) where it may be desirable to build from a limited set of visual elements to maintain a visual continuity of effect. Even when a grid is used it may still be necessary to make some changes to ensure optical consistency in the design.

Reproduction drawings and scale

Once a design has been approved and is ready to be drawn in its final form for reproduction, then a suitable scale must be chosen. There is no simple rule here because much depends on the range of sizes in which the mark is to be used and whether the working master is to be a photographic negative or perhaps a printed version. One simple way of selecting a scale is to determine the part of the design containing the finest detail or the junction of the thinnest lines and to choose a scale which allows this to be drawn with the minimum of technical difficulty.

Many designs require two or more master drawings; one for very small reduction, one for average sizes and one for large scale use. These will ensure that very thin lines do not disappear in the smallest size or become over-weighted in the largest display sizes. This is analogous to the modifications made to type designs over the whole range of point sizes. Further versions may be required for negative image use and for colour separation purposes as well as for more specialised uses such as stencil and illuminated treatments.

Optical corrections

I have already mentioned corrections for optical effects. They are basically the type of effects that we get in optical illusions. We may draw and intend a line to be vertical but because of a strong angular emphasis in some other part of the design the vertical may appear to lean to one side. The optical correction involves re-drawing the line to

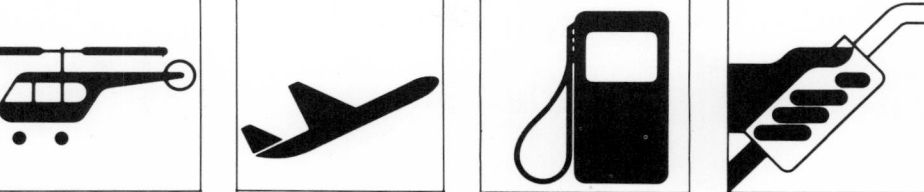

lean in the opposite direction to such an amount as to result in the line finally looking upright.

A change of viewing scale will often reveal the presence of this type of optical distortion.

One type of correction that often has to be made to a design is when one gets two lines or masses meeting at an acute angle resulting in a narrowing white gap ending in a fine point. In small scale reproduction, even photographic reproduction, this fine point will tend to fill in thus spoiling the effect of the sharp pointed shape. If the design is printed letterpress and is overinked and/or printed onto absorbent paper, this gap will tend to fill with ink and the whole effect of a sharp pointed shape will be lost. The solution is to allow for this 'filling in' effect by opening out the apex of the intersections (see illustration at bottom of page 27).

For many purposes a master drawing will be required showing the construction of the design. In its simplest form this can be shown on a simple grid but more complex designs will require a more detailed specification on which even the most subtle curves can be specified. Given the use of a calculator very complex ratios and divisions can be specified in conjunction with the metric scale. It should be remembered,

however, that some designs are required to be constructed either on a scale where hand tools cannot easily be used (see the note for the mark for the Sonja Henie-Neils Onstad Foundations, Oslo, 10/24 on page 119) or in situations where they may not be available.

Colour specification

When a colour or colours have to be specified in a national or international context we have the problem of finding common colour references, both between specifier and user, and between the types of colours used. Taking the latter point first: we may have to specify the same colour in both cellulose paint for, say, vehicles and in ink for one or more printing processes. One solution is to send out a basic colour sample, preferably in gloss, semi-matt and matt finishes, to be matched by all suppliers. Another solution is to make use of the Munsell colour system, the Pantone system, British Colour Standards or one of the proprietary paint or ink systems. Provided the same references are available at both ends, this is the simpler system and it enables exact colour references to be quoted by letter, telephone or telex. Each of these systems has its own advantages and limitations with the American Munsell system providing the greatest range of colours together with the facility of being able to specify colours not shown in the comprehensive Munsell colour dictionary.

37 (right)
From a set of pictograms designed by Braunstein & McLaren Associates based on the geometry of the grid shown at right. Only three line thicknesses have been used.
The upper set of pictograms were designed for cartographic purpose. The lower set were designed for signing the Lyon metro, France.

As in monochrome work, designs that are to appear in colour may require some optical correction to the basic drawing. An interesting example can be seen in the design of the five-ring International Olympic Committee emblem designed for the Munich Olympic Games (see illustration at bottom of page 26). This was drawn in two versions with different line weights, one for black and white use and one for the full five-colour version. The black and white version has circles of equal line width but the multi-coloured version has a different line width for each colour determined by the tonal weight of the colour.

Interference patterns

Perhaps a word should be said about those designs which make use of a series of parallel, converging, concentric or spiralling lines. When these are reproduced with certain screens or are scanned by a television camera a strong interference pattern may result through interaction of the design pattern and the reproduction screen. The resulting moiré pattern may not produce an unpleasant effect but it is wise to test a design of this type, particularly if it is to be shown on television.

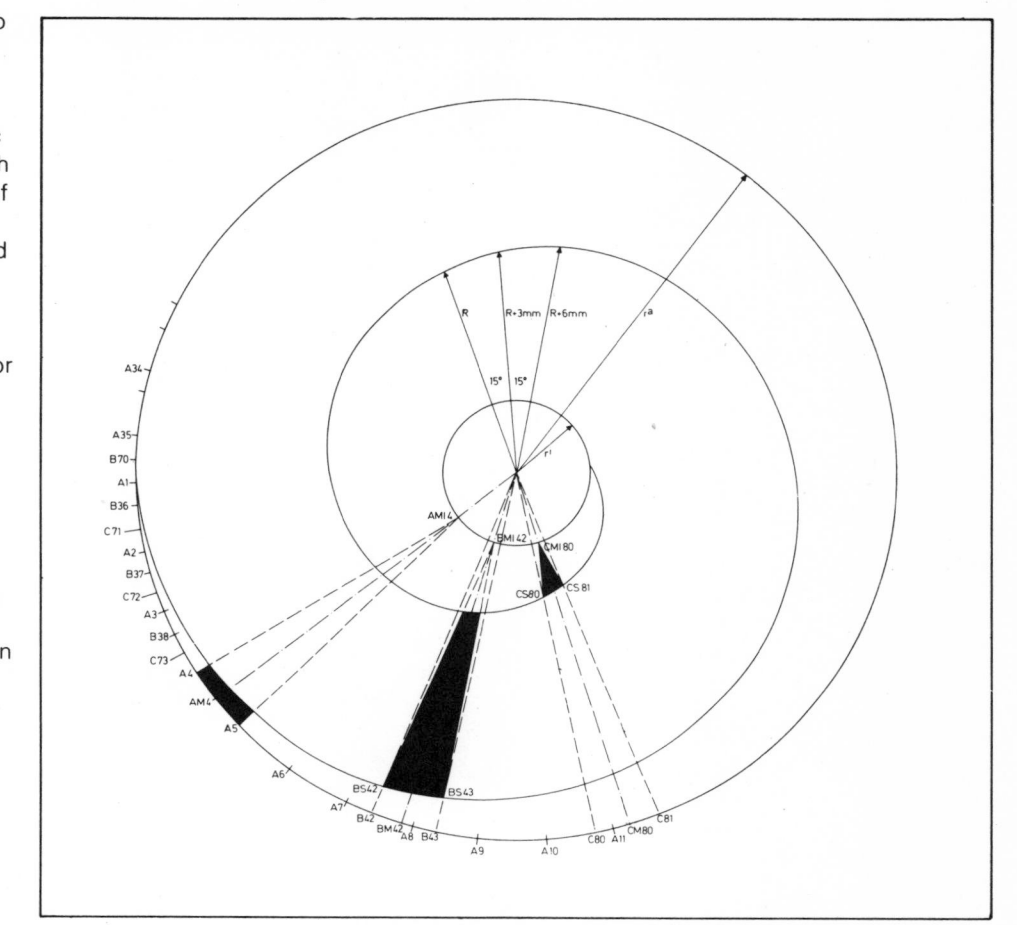

38
Construction drawing for the Munich
Olympic Games (see 9/20 on page 110).

39 (right)
Construction drawing by the author for a
mark for an electronics company based on
the letter M (project). Construction only
requires use of a calculator and a scale.

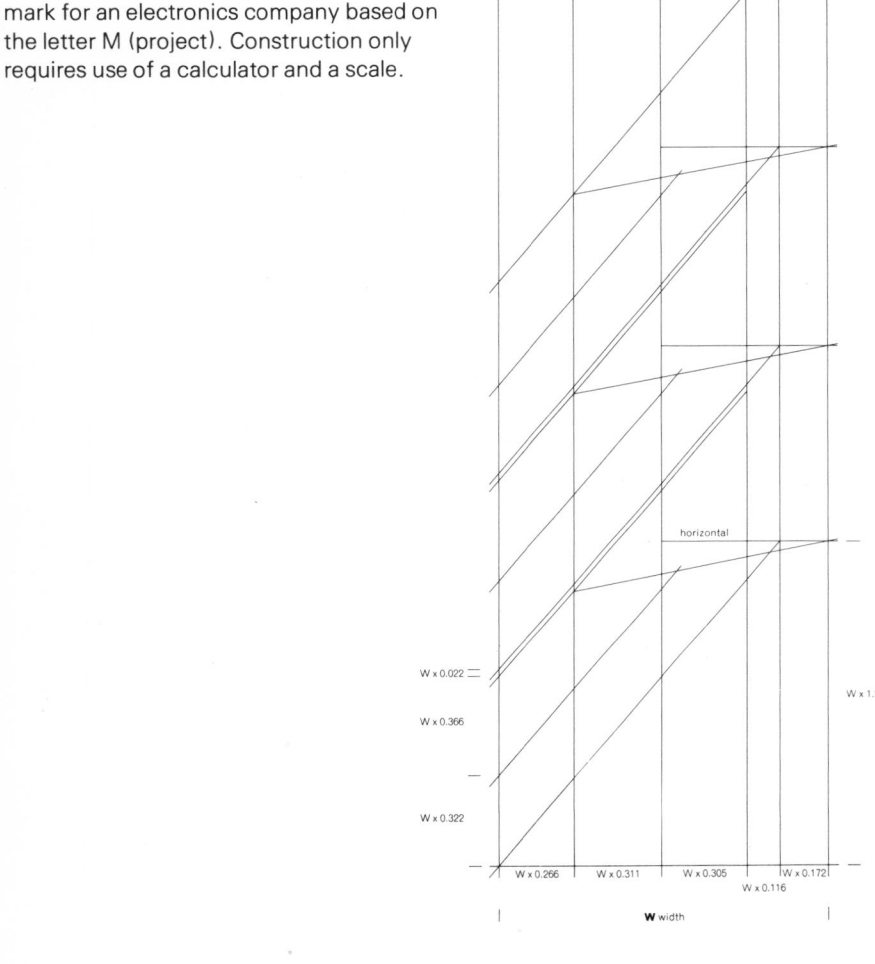

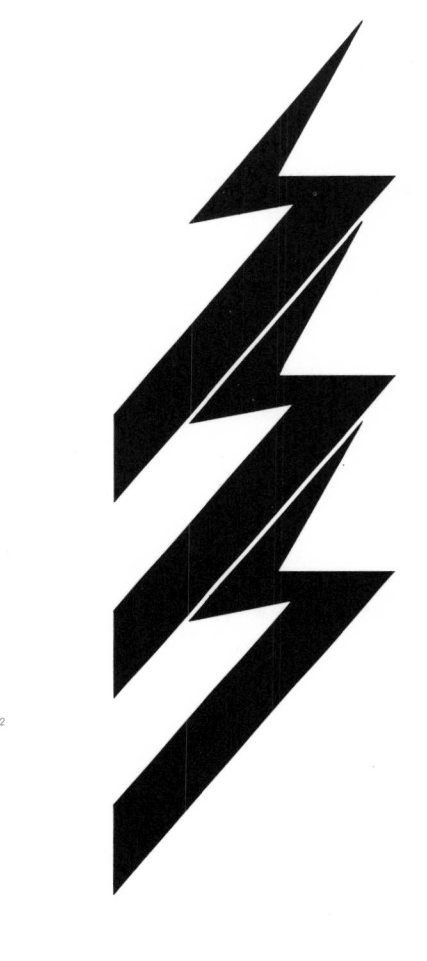

40 (right)
Trademark for Leeds Polytechnic designed
by T H B Russell MSIAD and P S Walker
(see 10/17 on page 117 for basic version of
this mark). Construction drawing of basic
unit and one of the possible groupings of the
unit.

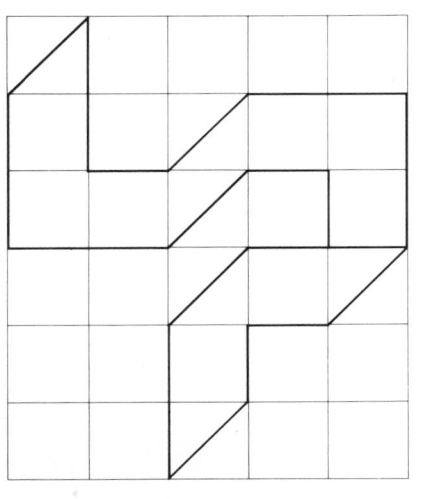

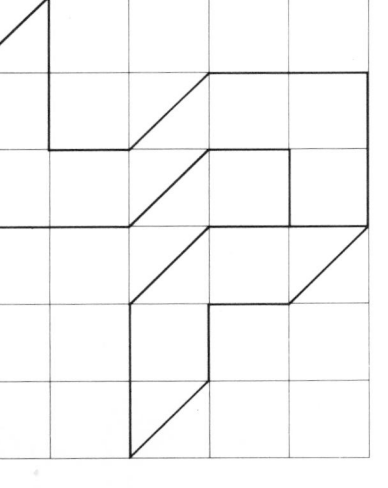

Some early forms of trademarks

Watermarks

Early wood engraving of a papermaker at work

Paper making first evolved in China about the beginning of the first century AD and the earliest forms were made from vegetable fibres in bamboo moulds. The secret of its production spread rapidly throughout Asia and was brought to Europe from Egypt and North Africa. Paper making in Spain and Italy is recorded in the 12th and 13th centuries and paper mills in other European countries soon followed. The earliest known watermark appears in an Italian paper made in Bologna in 1282. Papermaking in England dates from the end of the 15th century.

It was in Europe that the use of a fine wire mesh was developed in the paper making mould and it was the use of wire with its great flexibility that led to the invention of the watermark or more accurately the 'wiremark' since it is the wire impression that is implanted in the paper fibres during its production. The early papermakers' moulds were composed of a wooden frame supporting a matrix of fine parellel strands of wire which acted as a sieve in holding the macerated fibres after the water had been drained away (see early wood engraving at left). When dried and held up to the light the impression of these wires shows up as thin translucent 'laid' lines. If a simple design is made up out of wire and attached to this 'sieve' then it will also show up as an impression when viewed against the light. The constraint of producing a design from a length of wire without solid areas led to the characteristic linear nature of these early watermarks. The French term for a watermark, *un filigrane*, sums up very well the character of these early designs.

Early Watermarks were probably used to denote the maker or the location of the mill but were later used to denote the size and quality of a sheet. The Jester or Fool's Cap watermark, (see illustration) first seen about 1540, gave its name to the paper size of foolscap.

The fact that a watermark is indestructable has led both to its control for excise purposes and its use for many forms of security printing. This latter use has acted as a strong stimulus to produce more sophisticated forms of watermarking leading to coloured watermarks and shadow marks capable of rendering photographic tones.

Developments in technology may render the watermark obsolete for security purposes as paper can now be marked magnetically and it is of interest that developments in photography now allow us to photograph watermarks that were previously indecipherable through being covered by print or manuscript (the photographs below are examples of these beta-radiograph prints).

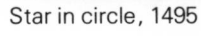

Negro head, Italy, c 1436   Star in circle, 1495   Bull, England 15th century

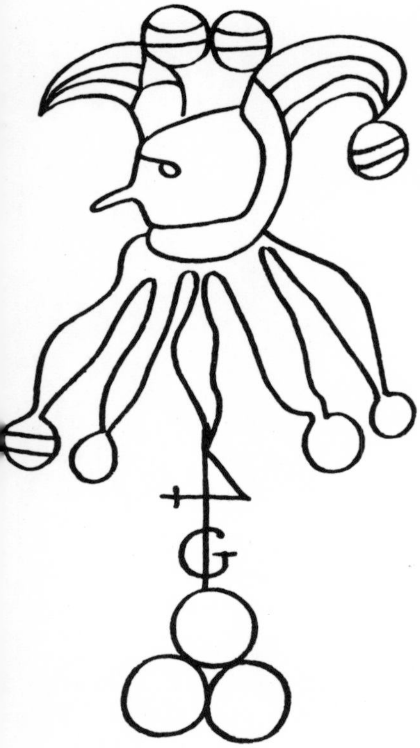

Foolscap, Rostoff, 1555

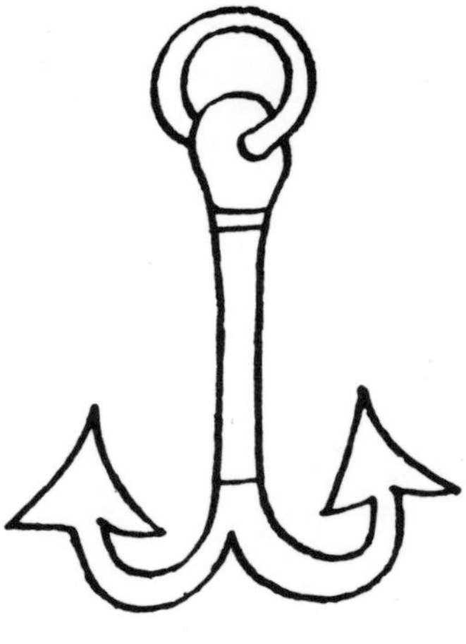

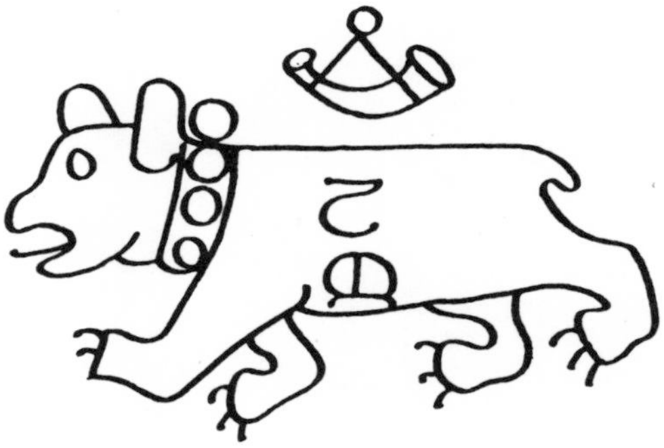

Anchor, Milan, Italy 1428
Bear, place of origin unknown, 1560

Watermark of a hand, Perigeuse, France
1540-50

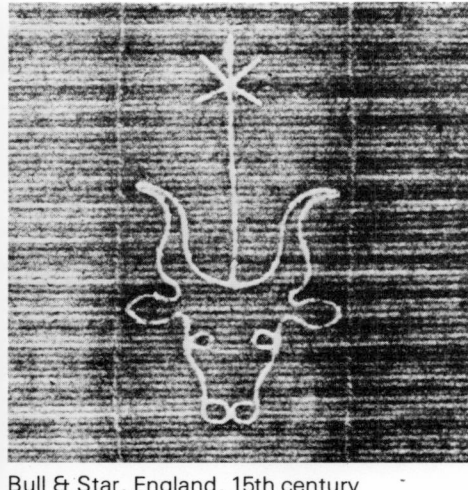

Bull & Star, England, 15th century

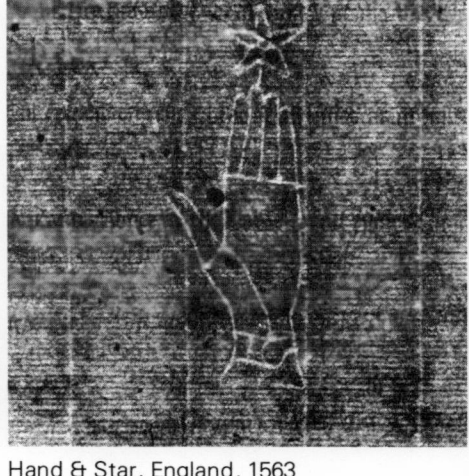

Hand & Star, England, 1563

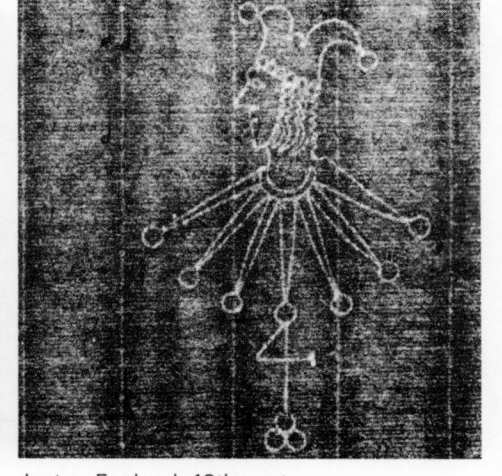

Jester, England, 18th century

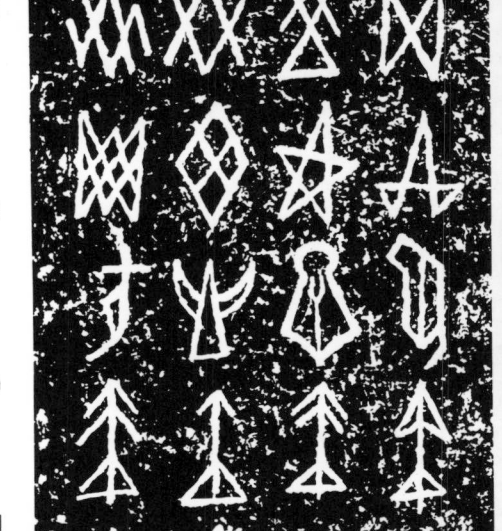

Merchants' marks

Merchants' marks were the direct forerunners of the modern trademark. They were in widespread use in Europe and this country from the end of the 13th century and were used originally to identify the owner of goods or the quality of his merchandise. Later on as trade guilds developed they identified membership of a guild or company and in certain trades the marks were registered and given protection by law. Some merchants used both a trade mark and an heraldic mark and there are some examples of a merchant mark appearing within an heraldic design.

These trading marks served to overcome the limitations of language both local and foreign at a time when there were few forms of printed matter and no mass produced containers by which the shape of the container could identify its owner. If we remember that each mark had to be repeated by hand, probably by brush, on each bale or container then we see that elaboration was difficult to achieve.

The marks were nearly always constructed around a vertical stem with the main elements at the top and base, and other elements flanking or crossing the centre.

The reason for this particular form and for its continuing use over several centuries is not clear but it has been suggested that the early marks were derived from the Runic alphabet.

Masons' marks from English churches

Mark of Richard Lant, bookbinder, on the cover of the Ipswich Domesday Book

Builders' mark from a house at Shrewsbury

Merchants' marks, 14th-17th century

Mark of William Caxton, 1422-1492, the first English printer

In this and the binding mark the owners' initials are assuming an equal importance with the trading mark and show the beginning of the departure from the earlier stylised forms

Hanseatic trading marks dating from 1406

Branding marks

Cattle branding, usually associated with the American West, was also quite common in Europe up to the beginning of this century. The nature of the mark and the painful method of application resulted in designs where distinctiveness and absolute economy of means were combined.

Many different types of animals and birds were marked to register ownership but one of the more interesting and best documented of these types of mark was that used to establish the ownership of swans. Swans have been kept in a semi-domesticised state in this country from about the 12th century, although these particular marks date from the 15th-17th centuries. The marks were inscribed on the upper mandible of the beak and a register of the marks was kept by a swan-master.

The marks have a strong visual link with merchants' marks of the same period, using a limited number of motifs and may be based on their owners' heraldic device.

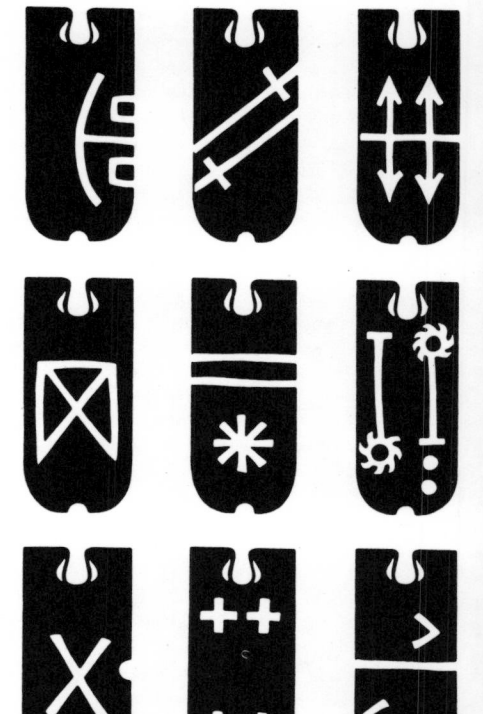

Swan marks from Lincolnshire and Suffolk, 15-17th centuries

Essex Forest cattle brands, 1908

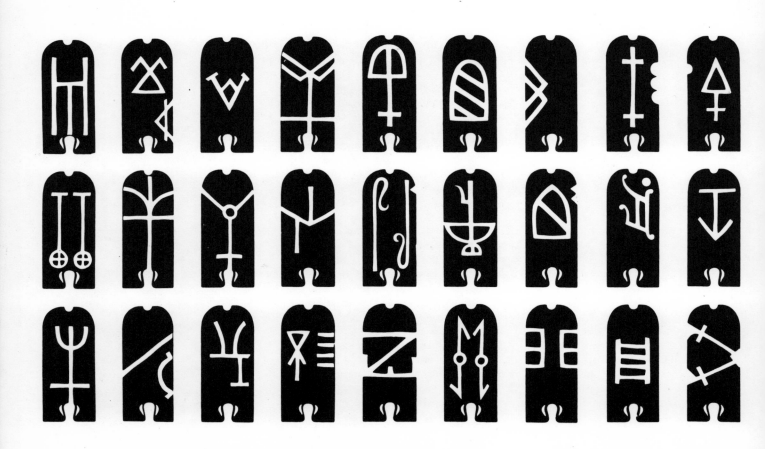

Suffolk and General; lead plate, seven-pointed star

Firemarks

Firemarks were a form of identification used by fire insurance companies from the late 1600's up to the beginning of this century. They were used to distinguish the properties insured by a particular company in the days when buildings were rarely numbered and precise addresses uncommon. The marks were attached to the outside of buildings, usually between the first floor windows and, to begin with, were cast from lead but at the beginning of the 19th century copper, tinned iron and brass were also used. Many of the marks were gilded and most painted in bright colours for maximum display value.

Following the great fire of London in 1666 a number of mutual fire insurance offices were set up and it was the fire insurance companies who for the next hundred and fifty years provided the local fire 'brigades'. It was not until 1866 that the Metropolitan Board of Works took over the London Fire Engine Establishment and it became a public undertaking.

Each company had its own design although there were often a number of variants produced and many of the marks included the policy number under the design. The image was often derived from the Company's name or location and rarely showed any direct connection with fire with the exception of the mythological designs for Phoenix Assurance and the Salamander & Western Fire Assurance. Most of the designs were bases on heraldic or patriotic motifs and it is the constraints of metal casting or embossing that give them a more vigorous quality compared with other contemporary printed designs.

Salamander & Western Fire Assurance Society, copper plates showing salamander in fire. (The lizard-like salamander was believed

to take the shape of a human and to go unscathed through fire)

Phoenix Assurance Company, phoenix rising from flames, tinned iron, c 1815

Protector Fire Insurance Company, copper
plate showing fireman and burning house,
c 1830.

Westminster Fire Office, lead plate, issued
before 1735

Leeds and Yorkshire Assurance Company,
copper plate, showing a ram's fleece,
c 1850

Above and at right
Sun Fire Office, lead plates, 1729

Fruit wrapping papers

These delightful citrus fruit wrapping papers are one of the most ephemeral of all printed matter, seldom surviving the unpacking of the fruit in the shop. Printed on thin white or coloured tissue paper their sole reason as marks is to identify a brand, a grower or a country. Many of the designs are true examples of folk art which have somehow survived the pressures of industrialisation. The majority of the fruit comes from southern countries: from Spain and Southern Italy, particularly Sicily, and from Israel and from other countries of the Middle East. The continuing use of individual wrappers is no doubt due to the difficulty of marking the textured surface of the fruit but they probably also help to retain the flavour.

The soft, unsized tissue has also contributed to the quality of these designs since the design must be relatively simple with open lines to allow for ink bleed. Many of the earlier designs appear to have been printed from, or inspired by, wood engraved blocks and it is possible that many of these wood blocks are still being used today. This is surely an example where the medium has contributed to the 'primitive' quality of the design and we can compare it to the elaborate multi-coloured cigar box labelling used since the early years of this century where the use of coated papers allowed full scope for more sophisticated reproduction techniques.

The imagery is taken from a wide variety of sources: fruit and sun, the methods of transport by ship or train, patriotic symbolism, heraldry and a number of geometric designs perhaps a distant reflection of Islamic patterns. Colours are always strong; predominantly blue and red with infillings of yellow, orange or gold but unfortunately black and white reproduction gives only a hint of their richness.

Tradesmen's cards

These trade cards were the early precursors of the trademark as we know it today. The use of the word 'card', however, is misleading as they were not the equivalent of our business card and were not, in fact, printed on card at all, but on good quality paper. Their size varied considerably but could be as large as 14″ x 8″ (356 x 203mm) and they served a dual purpose as advertisement and hand bill.

The early versions were printed from wood engraved blocks combined with hand set type, the imperfections of the metal type characters complementing the direct simplicity of the woodcut image. These wood engraved versions gave way to the more flexible copper engravings of the 18th Century in which the artist was able to integrate image and lettering in a way not previously possible.

Many of the images on these trademen's cards are derived from earlier shop signs. They have an appropriate simplicity and directness in showing the products or

services of their owner which was later lost in the elaboration and decorative use of the medium. It is interesting to note how the constraints of machine printing in the early nineteenth century, before the introduction of photographic reproduction, also led to a simpler, more direct form of image.

A T the Old Collier and Cart, at Fleet-Ditch, near Holborn-Bridge, Are good Coals, Deals, Wainscote and Beach, &c. sold at reasonable Rates, by
                    John Edwards.

All Sorts of Trumpetts and Kettle Drums ffrench: Hornes, Speaking Trumpetts Hearing Hornes for Deafe people & all Sorts of powder flasks and allso Wind Gunes made and minded by William Bull Trumpett maker to his Maiestie Who liveth att the Signe of the Trumpett and Horne in Castal Street Neare the Muyse.

Wardrobes bought
in Town & Country.

BY
JOHN FLUDE

Unredeemd Goods sold
Wholesale & Retail.

Money
Lent

Delegal Sculp.t Bishopsgate.

John Flude

PAWNBROKER and SILVERSMITH

N.º 2 Grace Church Street

London

Lends Money on Plate, Watches, Jewells, Wearing Apparel,
Houshold Goods, & Stock in Trade

NB

Goods Sent from any Part of ye Country directed as above,
shall be duly attended too & the Utmost Value lent thereon

James Potter,

Leather - Breeches Maker.

At the Sign of the Boot *and* Breeches, *within Three Doors of Aldgate, on the Left Hand Side of the Way, in* Shoemaker-Row.

Maketh and Selleth all Sorts of Leather-Breeches, by Wholesale and Retail, at Reasonable Rates. Likewise Buck and Doe Skins and all Sorts of Leather for Breeches.

Printed at the Old Katherine-Wheel without Bishopsgate

The Standard w.t of y Following Coins

		aw. gr.
Jacobus		6 = 6
Jacobus		3 = 3
Carolus		5 = 18
Carolus		2 = 21
Guinea		5 = 9
Guinea		2 = 16½
Moider		6 = 22½
Moider		3 = 11
Pistol		4 = 8
Pistol		2 = 4

Tim? Roberts at the Hand and Scales next y Corner of Queens Street in Watling Street LONDON, Makes & Sells all sorts of Scales, Weights, Stillards, & Cocks

Note, that Each Grain in Gold, is ½ at 4 p. Oun

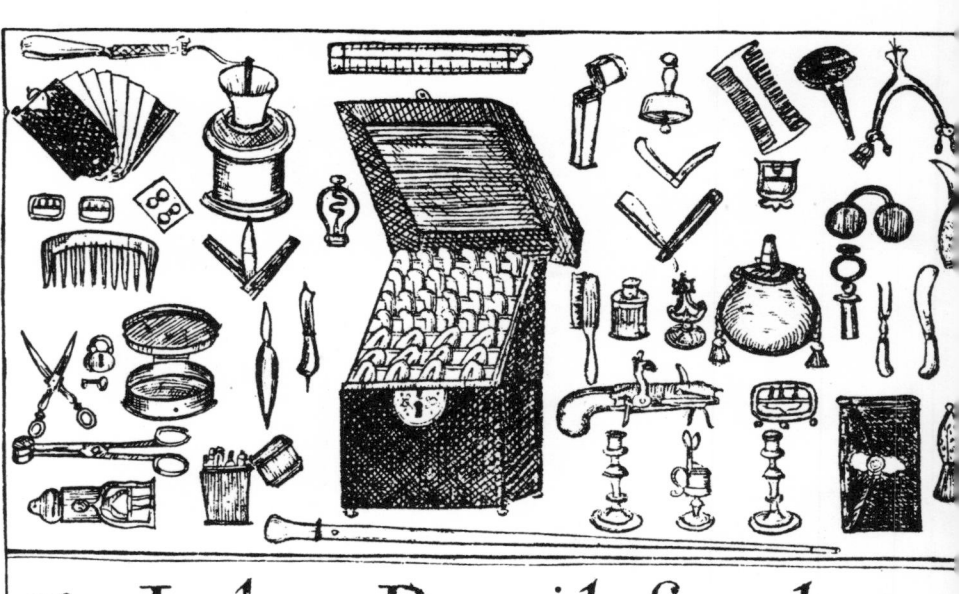

John Brailsford

CUTLER in y Broad part of St = Martins Court LEICESTER FIELDS maketh & Selleth all Sorts of the Best LONDON Work Knives Forks Razors Scissors Penknives fleams Gardners & Painters Knives Fine Steel & Mettle Buckels, Cork Screws Spurs Snuffers Tobacco & Snuff Boxes Powder Horns Dogs Collers & Padlocks Ivory Box & horn Combs Ivory Pocket Books & Brushes Canes Rules Pencils Curling Tongs Ink Stands &c with all Sorts of Birmingham & Sheffield Ware & Fitteth up Silver China & Aggett Hafts wth y best Steel Blades at Reasonable Rates. Canes Mounted

A collection of international trademark designs

A collection of international trademark designs

The trademarks in this section are assembled under ten different categories relating to the activities or services of their sponsors. This enables designs for related subjects to be easily compared. The subject matter of some of the marks is so wide that they overlap into more than one section and so an arbitary choice has had to be made in their grouping.

Wherever possible, trademarks that were designed for two-colour printing have been shown in two colours although not necessarily in the original colours.

The notes appearing underneath a mark are based on information supplied by the designer of the mark.

section	1	49	**Resources**
	2	53	**The environment**
	3	61	**Transportation**
	4	67	**Industry**
	5	75	**Products**
	6	83	**The high street**
	7	89	**Services**
	8	99	**Communications**
	9	105	**Entertainment & sport**
	10	113	**Organisations & societies**

1/1
Alireza Group of Companies, Kuwait
(Supplies back-up services to the oil
companies, construction rigs, pipelines,
tanks, &c)
Designer/Tor Pettersen, Lock/Pettersen
Ltd, London

The design is a pictograph of oil rigs

1/2
Itaipu Binacional
(Hydro-electric plant)
Designer/Aloisio Magalhães, Rio de Janeiro,
Brazil

This hydro-electric plant is located on
the Brazil-Paraguay border with equal
participation by both countries. It was
therefore designed as a symmetrical form
based on the mirror image of the letter 'i'

1/3
Furnas Centrais Elétricas SA
(Power company)
Designers/Joaquim Redig and Rafael
Rodrigues, Rio de Janeiro, Brazil

Former symbol was a realistic representation
of a transmission pylon. New mark is made
up of two overlapping five-pointed stars with
linear variations

1/4
John Wainwright & Co Ltd
(Basalt quarries)
Designer/Roger Simmons NDD, MSIAD,
Bath, England

1/5
Kuwait National Petroleum Company
(Oil and petroleum products)
Designer/Alan Fletcher, Pentagram, London

Initials designed specifically for use as a
petrol station sign.

/6
cott Energy Systems
(Supplier of home heating oil)
Designer/Joe Selame, Massachusetts, USA

Original colours: red and brown

/7
Oil Tools Ltd
(Suppliers of equipment for oil exploration
and recovery companies)
Designer/Michael Pacey, Vancouver, BC,
Canada

1/8
New Gold Star Mines
(Mining, smelting and processing)
Designer/Michael Pacey, Vancouver, BC,
Canada

1/9
Grupo Paraiso
(Cement manufacturer)
Designer/Roberto Lanari, Rio de Janeiro,
Brazil

Mark at bottom shows an alternative design

1/10
Söll
(Steel works)
Designer/Anton Stankowski, Stuttgart,
Germany

1/11
Oakhurst Farms
Designer/Ernst Roch Design
Montreal, Canada

1/12
Sheerness Steel
(Steel company)
Designer/Lippincott & Margulies, London

1/13
**The International Nickel Company of
Canada Ltd**
(Base metal industry)
Designer/Hans Kleefeld, Stewart and
Morrison Ltd, Toronto, Canada

1/14
British Steel Corporation
Designer/David Gentleman, London

2/1
Soler Lavernia
(Building construction)
Designer/Francesc Guitart, Barcelona,
Spain

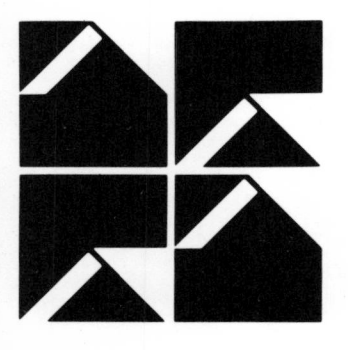

2/2
Town Centre, Marathon Realty Co Ltd
(Shopping plaza development)
Designer/Alistair Justason, Stewart &
Morrison, Toronto, Canada

2/3
Lea Valley Regional Park Authority
(A recreational park)
Designer/David Lock, Lock Pettersen Ltd,
London

2/4
Glen Abbey Community
(A new town development)
Designer/Malcolm Waddell, Gottschalk &
Ash Ltd, Toronto, Canada

Original colours: blue (top) yellow and green

2/5
Scarborough Town Centre
(A civic and shopping centre)
Designer/Hans Kleefeld, Stewart &
Morrison, Toronto, Canada

2/6
Land Hessen
(Industrial estate)
Designer/Anton Stankowski, Stuttgart,
West Germany

2/7
York Centre
(Office building/shopping arcade)
Designer/Stuart Ash, Gottschalk & Ash Ltd,
Toronto, Canada

2/8
Société de Développement de la Baie James
(Development scheme)
Designer/Peter Hablutzel, Cabana, Séquin
Inc, Montreal, Canada

The marks below identify various aspects of
the scheme: petroleum, energy,
telecommunications, forests and mines

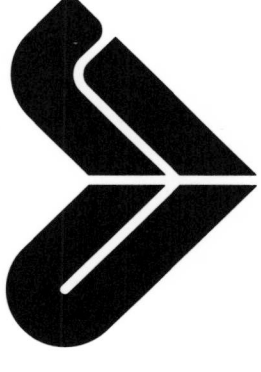

2/9
Deschamps Excavation Inc.
(General excavation activities for
construction work)
Designer/Raymond Bellemare, Quebec,
Canada

2/10
**Metropolitan Toronto & Region
Conservation Authority**
(Operation of conservation areas)
Designer/Glen Arnold, Stewart & Morrison
Ltd, Toronto, Canada

2/11
Construction Queiroz Galvão
(Road construction)
Designer/Joaquim Redig, Rio de Janeiro,
Brazil

2/12
Schwihag GMBH
(Railway planning and construction)
Designer/Wolfgang Heuwinkel, Bergisch
Gladbach, West Germany

2/13
Saint-en-Yvelines
(New town development in France)
Designer/Kinneir Calvert Tuhill, London

Part of an information programme for a new
town. Photograph shows SQ emblem used
as a boundary marker

2/14
National Water Council
(National body controlling the many uses of
water)
Designer/Banks and Miles, London

Original colours: green, dark blue-green,
green

2/15
Aberdeen Harbour Board
(Management of all habour facilities in
Aberdeen)
Designer/Albert Brebner, Edinburgh,
Scotland

2/16
**Servienge, Companhia Serviços de
Engenharia**
(Road construction)
Designer/Joaquim Redig, Rio de Janeiro,
Brazil

The mark is based on the concept of contour
lines

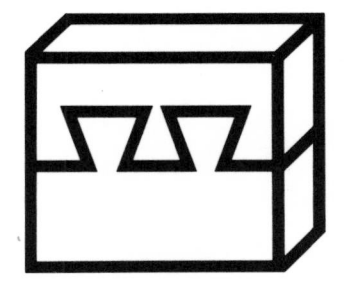

2/17
Gemeinnützige Siedlungsgesellschaft Gronauer Wald
(Communal housing company)
Designer/Wolfgang Heuwinkel, Bergisch
Gladbach, West Germany

2/18 (and at right)
Tom Sim Ltd
(Building design and joinery)
Designer/Peter Nutter, Thumb Design
Partnership, London

Two related marks reflecting the two areas
of the company's work

2/19
Isseks Brothers Inc.
(Water tanks)
Designer/Robert P. Gersin, New York

2/20
bv Bouwbedrijf Hazenberg
(Building contractors)
Designer/Wim van der Weerd, T D Associati
voor Total Design bv, Amsterdam, Holland

/21
homas Warrington & Sons Ltd
Building contractor and property developer)
Designer/Derek J Waterfield, Stockport,
ngland

/22
Gebr. Van Heeswyk
Building contractors)
Designer/Ben Bos, TD Associatie voor Total
Design bv, Amsterdam, Holland

2/23
William Bloom & Son Incorporated
(Manufacturer of microstructures and space
enclosure systems)
Designer/Ronald Jacob, New Mexico, USA

2/24
Holroyd Construction Ltd
(Building construction, plant hire and
constructional engineering)
Designer/Keith Murgatroyd, Royle-
Murgatroyd Design Associates Ltd, London

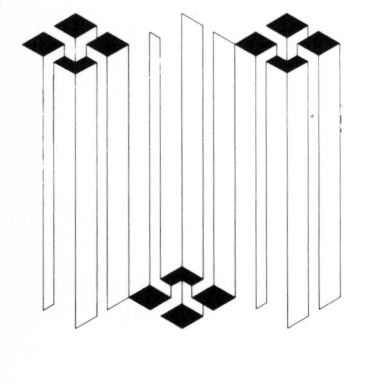

2/25
Nueva Linea
(Building components)
Designer/Francesc Guitart, Barcelona,
Spain

2/26
**Star Holdings, English Property
Corporation Ltd**
(Property investment and development)
Designer/Peter Ward, Ward Meredith
Associates, London

A 'star' emblem with architectural
associations

2/27
Imobiliária Novo Mundo
(Building construction)
Designer/Joaquim Redig, Rio de Janeiro,
Brazil

2/28
Norcount Realty Control Corporation
(Property management)
Designer/Stuart Ash, Gottschalk & Ash Ltd
Toronto, Canada

3/1
Ontario Trucking Association
(Association of trucking companies)
Designer/Peter Adam, Gottschalk & Ash,
Toronto, Canada

3/2
Hong Kong Air International Ltd
(Helicopter transport)
Designer/Henry Steiner, Graphic Com-
munication Ltd, Hong Kong

3/3
National Bus Company
(Express coaches and stage carriage buses
Designer/Norman Wilson FSIAD,
Manchester, England

A two-colour version in red (top) and blue is
used on National Express coaches and a
single colour version on buses

3/4
Flughafen
(Competition for an airport symbol)
Designer/Anton Stankowski, Stuttgart,
West Germany

3/5
British Airways
Designer/Negus & Negus, London

The flight symbol is evolved from the Union flag and its original colours are blue (the triangle) and red

3/6
Hong Kong Air International Ltd
(Air transport)
Designer/Henry Steiner, Graphic Communication Ltd, Hong Kong

3/7
Rockwell International
(International corporation whose field of activities include aircraft and spacecraft manufacture, transportation, nuclear and other energy sources, defence systems and electronics)
Designer/Saul Bass & Associates Inc, Los Angeles, USA

3/8
Loganair
(Scottish Airline including scheduled services, oil support, charter and air ambulance work)
Designer/Charles S Randak, Randak Design Consultants, Glasgow, Scotland

The mark incorporates the 'L' of Loganair and is intended to suggest the short takeoff and landing capabilities of the aircraft used

3/9
Docenave, Vale do Rio Doce Navegação SA
(Shipping company)
Designer/Aloisio Magalhães, Rio de Janeiro, Brazil

3/10
Aeroport de Paris
Designer/Adrian Frutiger, France

3/11
Sudbury Transit
(Municipal bus system)
Designer/Stuart Ash, Gottschalk & Ash,
Toronto, Canada

3/12
Société des Autoroutes du Sud de La France
Designer/Brigitte Rousset, Atelier Frutiger,
Arcueil, France

3/13
Oakville Transit
(Municipal bus system)
Designer/Stuart Ash, Gottschalk & Ash,
Toronto, Canada

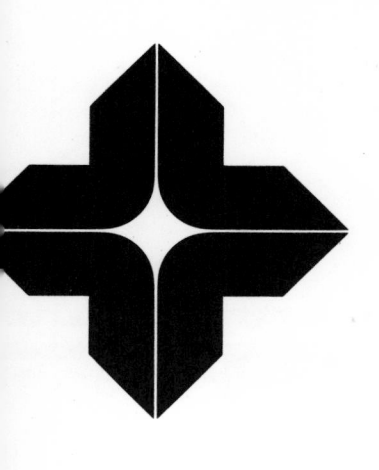

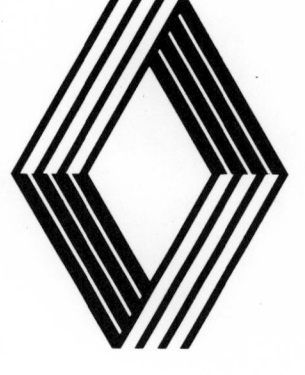

3/14
**La Commission de Transport de La Ville
de Laval**
(Public transport commission)
Designer/Georges Huel, Montreal, Canada

3/15
Chrysler International
(Vehicle manufacturer)
Designer/not known

3/16
Citroën
(Vehicle manufacturer)
Designer/not known

3/17
Régie Nationale des Usines Renault
(Renault cars)
Designer/Victor Vasarely, Paris

3/18
Rutan Transport Inc.
(Freight transport)
Designer/Raymond Bellemare, Quebec,
Canada

3/19
Overseas Containers Ltd
(Shipping)
Designers/John Harrison and Stephen
Smith, Stewart Morrison Harrison Ltd,
London

A mark designed to read on both smooth
and corrugated shipping containers

3/20
Hull & Humber Cargo Handling Co Ltd
(Stevedoring and forwarding agents)
Designer/Eurographic Ltd, Hull, England

3/21
**Transtec International Freight Services
Ltd**
(International freighting)
Designer/David Lock, Lock Pettersen Ltd,
London

The original colours are red stripes on a
strong yellow background

3/22
Bulgarische Staatseisenbahnen
(State railway)
Designer/Stephan Kantscheff, Sofia,
Bulgaria

First prize in a competition

4/1
Pausa Mössingen
(Textile printing works)
Designer/Anton Stankowski, Stuttgart,
West Germany

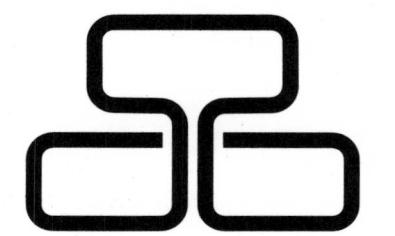

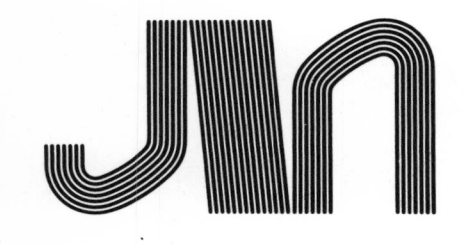

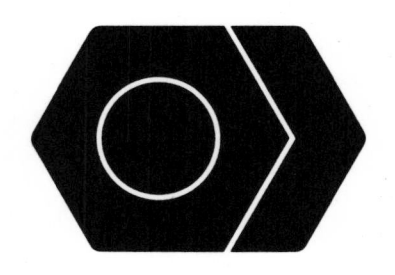

4/2
Johnson & Nephew Group
(Industrial wire manufacturer)
Designer/John Harrison, Stewart Morrison
Harrison, London

Colours: brown and grey

4/3
Howard Machinery
(Manufacturers of agricultural machinery)
Designer/Lippincott & Margulies, London

4/4
British Industrial Holdings
(Heavy duty engineering and industrial
product group)
Designer/John Harrison, Stewart Morrison
Harrison Ltd, London

Colours: black and dark blue

4/5
Irish Flock
(Manufacturers of springs for car seating)
Designer/George Daulby, London

4/6
CompAir Ltd
(Compressed air engineering)
Designer/Michael Tucker, Michael Tucker &
Associates, London

4/7
Stella Meta Filters Ltd
Designer/Tor Pettersen, Lock Pettersen Ltd,
London

(Project) The mark symbolises pressure
filters and shows the liquid flow as in the
filters themselves

4/8
Lucas Industries
(Manufacturers and distributors of auto-
motive parts and equipment, with related
activity in the aerospace, defence systems
and marine industries)
Designers/Colin Forbes, Alan Fletcher,
Pentagram, London

The diagonal mark can be reproduced in any
length and acts as an element of
identification for all group companies

4/9
AJ Parsons & Sons Ltd
(Air brake specialists for commercial
vehicles)
Design/Roger Simmons NDD, MSIAD

4/10
Delanair Ltd
(Manufacturer of car heating and ventilating
systems)
Designer/Tor Pettersen, Lock Pettersen Ltd,
London

4/11
James A Jobling Ltd
(Glass manufacturers)
Designer/Lippincott & Margulies, London

4/12
Reed Paper Limited
(Canadian and American manufacturer of
paper, paper products, furniture and
chemicals)
Designer/Burton Kramer, Burton Kramer
Associates Limited, Toronto, Canada

4/13
FBG Trident
(An amalgamation of two old established
glass manufacturing companies)
Designer/Banks and Miles, London

4/14
Medicelectrica
(Electrical equipment for medical use)
Designer/Félix Beltrán, Havana, Cuba

4/15
Cape Boards & Panels Ltd
(Manufacturers of fireproof wallboards and
ceiling panels)
Designer/Jean Robert
Pentagram, London

Colour: flame red

4/16
Yue Sang Engineering Ltd
(Fire protection services)
Designer/Hon Bing Wah, Hong Kong

4/17
The Technitron Group
(Electronics)
Designer/Robert P Gersin, New York

4/18
Unilever International
Designer/Collis Clements, Kent, England

4/19
John Heyer Paper Ltd
(Paper and packaging materials)
Designer/Wolfgang Heuwinkel, Bergisch
Gladbach, West Germany

4/20
VEB Kalksandsteinwerk Elsterwerda
Designer/Dieter Nemitz, Cottbus, DDR

4/21
Benz AG
(Timber merchant)
Designer/Rosmarie Tissi, Atelier Odermatt
& Tissi, Zurich, Switzerland

4/22
Schelling Wellpappen AG
(Manufacturers of corrugated card and
paper for packaging)
Designer/Siegfried Odermatt, Odermatt &
Tissi, Zurich, Switzerland

4/23
Reginald Bennett Limited
(Machinery importers)
Designer/Stuart Ash, Gottschalk & Ash
Limited, Toronto, Canada

4/24
Elton
(Electrical products)
Designer/Jan Hollender, Warsaw, Poland

4/25
Essilor International
(Optical glass and precision instrument
manufacturer)
Designer/Jean Widmer, Paris

4/26
Consolidated Foods Inc.
Designer/Landor Associates, California,
USA

4/27
Sandell Perkins
(Wood merchants)
Designer/Peter Gauld, Kent, England

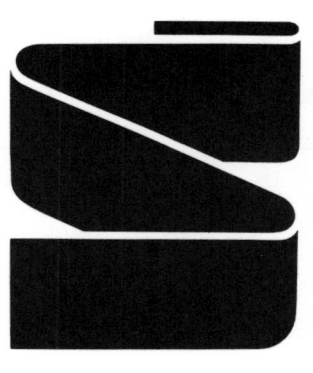

4/28
Reunion Nacional de Investigacion
(Chemistry research)
Designer/Félix Beltrán, Havana, Cuba

4/29
Royer, Royer, Thivierge
(Structural engineers)
Designer/Claude A Simmard, Quebec,
Canada

4/30
SWIT
(Paper industry)
Designer/Jaroslaw Jasinski, Warsaw,
Poland

4/31
Mackarl Electronics Inc.
Designer/Henry Steiner, Graphic
Communication Ltd, Hong Kong

5/1
Chelsea Drug & Chemical Company
(Pharmaceutical manufacturers)
Designer/Tor Pettersen, Lock Pettersen Ltd,
London

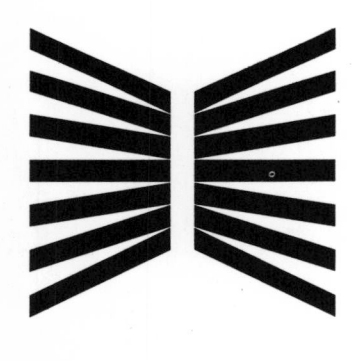

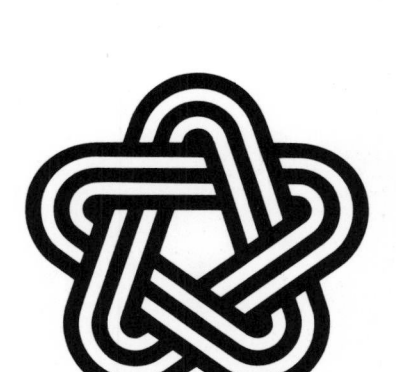

5/2
Imasco Ltd
(Parent company of a group of corporations producing high quality consumer goods)
Designer/Rolf Harder,
Montreal, Canada

5/3
Co-operative of Disabled Workmen in Stupsk, Poland
(Knitwear)
Designer/Jaroslaw Jasinski, Warsaw, Poland

5/4
Uspech-Sofia
(Ceramic manufacturer)
Designer/Stephan Kantscheff, Sofia, Bulgaria

5/5
Francine Vandeluc Tricots
(Machine knitwear)
Designer/Raymond Bellemare, Quebec, Canada

Mark based on the letter 'V' and knitting stitch

5/6
Funfstrahl-Stadt Sewliewo
(Textiles)
Designer/Stephan Kantscheff, Sofia, Bulgaria

/7
Champlain Container Corporation, USA
(Box and carton manufacturer)
Designer/Stuart Ash, Gottschalk & Ash,
Toronto, Canada

5/8
Queenswear (Canada) Ltd
(Clothing)
Designer/Rolf Harder,
Montreal, Canada

5/9
Mettler & Co Ltd
(Textiles)
Designer/Rosmarie Tissi, Atelier Odermatt
& Tissi, Zurich, Switzerland

5/10
Castagna Arredamenti
(Furniture manufacturer)
Designer/Rinaldo Cutini, Rome, Italy

5/11
Polyzathe BV
(Project development)
Designer/Jurriaan Schrofer, TD Associatie
voor Total Design bv, Amsterdam, Holland

5/12
Alarma
(Electronic alarm equipment)
Designer/Ben Bos, TD Associatie voor Total
Design bv, Amsterdam, Holland

5/13
Wallis Laboratories
(Tablet manufacturers)
Designer/David Lock and Tor Pettersen,
Lock Pettersen Ltd, London

5/14
Living Aids Ltd
(Makers of furniture and apparatus to assist
the disabled)
Designer/Walter Bernardini MSIAD, MSDI,
Dublin, Ireland

5/15
John Wilson (Twines) Ltd
Designer/Albert Brebner, Edinburgh,
Scotland

5/16
Dieter Kiekbusch
(Breeder of exotic birds)
Designer/Herbert Prüget, Berlin, DDR

5/17
Quick Maid Rental Services Ltd
(Vending machine manufacturers)
Designer/Ken Garland and Associates,
London

5/18
Central Sewing Machine Inc.
Designer/Denis L'Allier, Montreal, Canada

5/19
Travel bag factory in Zgorzelec, Poland
Designer/ Roman Rosyk, Wroclaw, Poland

5/20
**Leather Factory 'Pezos' in Stupsk,
Poland**
(Shoe manufacturer)
Designer/Jaroslaw Jasinski, Warsaw,
Poland

5/21
Abitibi Provincial Paper
(Manufacturers of fine papers)
Designer/Robert Burns, Toronto, Canada

A product mark to identify papers containing
recycled fibre, incorporating the letter 'A' in
a mobius continuum

5/22
Cyrmac Plastics Inc
(Plastic containers)
Designer/Raymond Bellemare, Quebec,
Canada

5/23
Tonsos Stadt Jambol
(Jacquard tapestry manufacturers)
Designer/Stephan Kantscheff, Sofia,
Bulgaria

5/24
**Small Industries Council for Rural Areas
of Scotland**
(Government department promoting all craft
industries in Scotland)
Designer/Albert Brebner, Edinburgh,
Scotland

The mark changes colour each year

/25
Maude Neon Industries Ltd
(Outdoor advertising and sign manufacturer)
Designers/Stuart Ash, Fredy Jaggie, Fritz
Gottschalk, Gottschalk & Ash Ltd, Toronto,
Canada

Alternative versions of the mark are also
shown

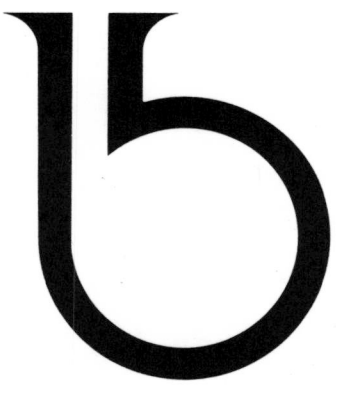

5/26
Lamper
(Tubular metal furniture manufacturer)
Designer/F. Guitart, Barcelona, Spain

5/27
Statler Tissue Corporation
(Manufacturer of toilet and facial tissues)
Designer/Joe Selame, Selame Design,
Massachusetts, USA

5/28
Biode Pharmaceutical Industries Ltd
Designer/Tor Pettersen, Lock Pettersen Ltd,
London

5/29
Ulster Carpets
Designers/Ivan and Robin Dodd, London

5/30
**Co-operative of Disabled Workmen
'Jedność' in Grójec, Poland**
(Fruit, confectionery)
Designer/Jaroslaw Jasinski, Warsaw,
Poland

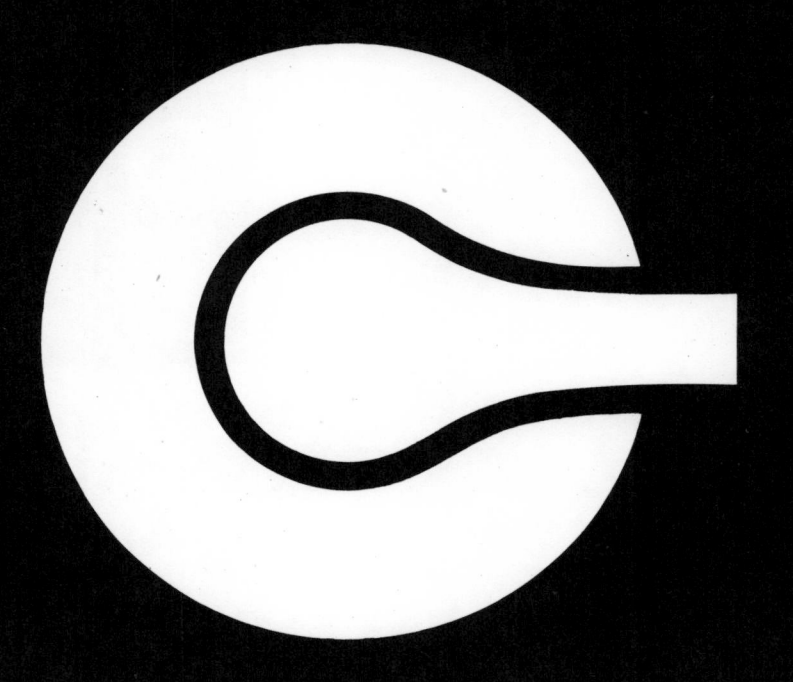

6/1
Pharmacie Centre
(Chemist)
Designer/Ernst Roch, Roch Design,
Montreal, Canada

6/2
Crosby Books
(Bookseller)
Designer/Negus & Negus, London

6/3
A. Graff
(Bookdealer)
Designer/Peter Riefenstahl, Braunschweig,
Germany

6/4
Kytta
(Pharmaceutical products)
Designer/Anton Stankowski, Stuttgart,
West Germany

6/5
H. Prückel
(Diamond merchant)
Designer/Rosmarie Tissi, Atelier Odermatt
& Tissi, Zurich, Switzerland

6/6
Points East
(Restaurant)
Designer/Glen Arnold, Stewart & Morrison
Ltd, Toronto, Canada

6/7
Ber Gold Inc.
(Jewelry importers)
Designer/Stuart Ash, Gottschalk & Ash
Limited, Toronto, Canada

6/8
The Four C's Aviaries Ltd
Designer/Glenn Tutssel, London

6/9
Reilly Lock Corporation Ltd
(Locksmiths)
Designer/Stuart Ash, Gottschalk & Ash Ltd,
Toronto, Canada

6/10
Libreria Borghese
(Bookshop)
Designer/Rinaldo Cutini, Rome, Italy

6/11
Apotheke Sammet
(Chemist)
Designer/Siegfried Odermatt, Odermatt &
Tissi, Zurich, Switzerland

6/12
Ursula
(Flower shop)
Designer/Félix Beltrán AGI, Havana, Cuba

6/13
Rug Tufters Inc.
(Handicraft company)
Designer/Peter Adam, Gottschalk & Ash
Limited, Toronto, Canada

6/14
Spadaro Ventura SPA
(Pharmaceutical company)
Designer/Rinaldo Cutini, Rome, Italy

Colours: green and black

6/15
Arflex
(Interior design)
Designer/Giancarlo Iliprandi, Milan, Italy

6/16
Backerei Burkhardt Volketswil
(Bakery)
Designer/Rosmarie Tissi, Atelier Odermatt
& Tissi, Zurich, Switzerland

6/17
Colonial Provision Company Inc.
(Manufacturer of meat products)
Designer/Joe Selame, Massachusetts, USA

6/18
De Gruyter
(Supermarket chain)
Designer/Wim van der Weerd, TD
Associatie voor Total Design bv,
Amsterdam, Holland

6/19
Gebrüder Heinemann
(Duty-free shops in airports and on ships)
Designer/Alan Fletcher, Pentagram, London

6/20
Sound Investment
(Stereo tapes and components)
Designer/Michael Pacey, Vancouver, BC,
Canada

6/21
Stewarts Supermarkets (Belfast) Ltd
Designer/Richard Daynes FSIAD, London

6/22
Milton Laundry
Designer/Ken Vail, Ken Vail Graphic Design,
Cambridge, England

6/23
The Wine Attic
(Retail store for wine making)
Designer/Jürgen Hoffman, Halifax, Nova
Scotia, Canada

6/24
Marcello Masi
(Distributor of office machines)
Designer/Rinaldo Cutini, Rome, Italy

7/1
Occulenti
(Contact lenses)
Designer/John Stegmeijer, Amsterdam,
Holland

7/2
State National Bank of El Paso
(Banking and bank related services)
Designer/Landor Associates, California,
USA

7/3
**Compagnie Financière et du Crédit SA,
Switzerland**
(Banking and finance)
Designer/David Gentleman, London

7/4
National Westminster Bank Group
Designers/Hewat, Swift, Walters Ltd,
London

7/5
Canada Systems Group
(Computer programming and computer
systems)
Designer/Burton Kramer, Burton Kramer
Associates Limited, Toronto, Canada

/6
**Helix Investments
Venture Capital Corporation**
Designer/Robert Burns, Toronto, Canada

/7
Banco Mercantil de Pernambuco
(Bank)
Designer/Aloisio Magalhães, Rio de Janeiro,
Brazil

7/8
Friesland Bank
Designer/Wim Crouwel, TD Associatie voor
Total Design bv, Amsterdam, Holland

7/9
Jardine Fleming & Co Ltd
(Financial and investment advisors)
Designer/Henry Steiner, Graphic
Communication Ltd, Hong Kong

7/10
Grupo Nacional
(Banking group)
Designer/Aloisio Magalhães, Rio de Janeiro,
Brazil

7/11
Urbana Insieme SRL
(Building society)
Designer/Michele Spera, Roma, Italy

7/12
Central Office of Information Training Services Agency
(Commercial and industrial retraining)
Designers/June Fraser and Mike Butts, Design Research Unit, London

7/13
Stadtsparkasse Köln
(Competition for Cologne Municipal Savings Bank)
Designer/Anton Stankowski, Stuttgart, West Germany

7/14
Applied Research and Management Co
Designer/Louis-André Rivard, Montreal, Canada

7/15
Selection Thomson Ltd
(Management selection consultants)
Designer/Albert Brebner, Edinburgh, Scotland

7/16
e Nordet Inc.
Production managers for artists)
esigner/Raymond Bellemare, Quebec,
anada

7/17
Overseas Computer Consultants
Designer/Peter Wildbur, London

7/18
Maritime Computers Ltd
(Computer services)
Designer/Jürgen Hoffman, Halifax,
Nova Scotia,

7/19
McLair Nicol Associates
(Computer programmers)
Designer/Albert Brebner, Edinburgh,
Scotland

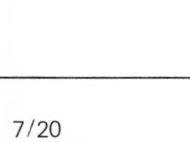

7/20
The Graphic Statement
(Design and illustration studio)
Designer/Michael Pacey, Vancouver, BC,
Canada

7/21
Bonaria Casu
(Design and public relations)
Designer/Rinaldo Cutini, Rome, Italy

7/22
Raymond Bellemare
(Designer's own mark)
Designer/Raymond Bellemare, Quebec,
Canada

7/23
Interlabor SA
(Employment Agency)
Designer/Ben Bos, TD Associatie Total
Design bv, Amsterdam, Holland

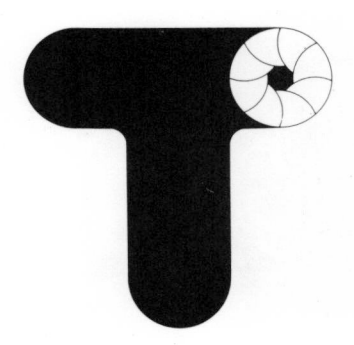

/24
T Bolton
Printer)
Designer/Jonathan De Morgan
Leeds, England

Design basis: letter B and process halftone
dot

/25
C I Designs Inc.
Contract furniture manufacture and sales)
Designer/Hauser Associates Inc. Georgia,
USA

7/26
Adolfo Tomeucci
(Photographer)
Designer/Rinaldo Cutini, Rome, Italy

7/27
Communikart Inc.
(Graphic design)
Designer/Claude A Simard, Quebec,
Canada

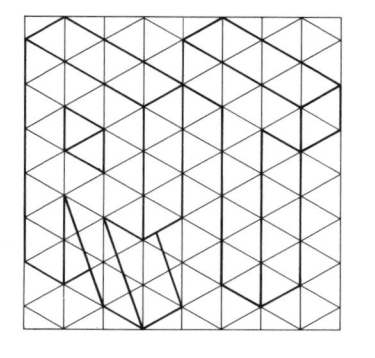

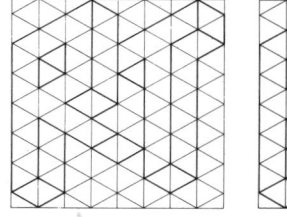

7/28
Luis Lapidus
(Architect)
Designer / Félix Beltrán, Havana, Cuba

7/29 (and at right)
Rock Townsend
(Architects, planners, designers)
Designer / Alan Fletcher, Pentagram, London

One of several variations of the logotype
based on the letters RT within a grid

7/30
**DI Design & Development
Consultants Ltd**
(Architectural and interior design
consultants)
Designer / Stuart Ash, Gottschalk & Ash Ltd,
Toronto, Canada

7/31
Enric Graells
(Architects)
Designer / Francesc Guitart, Barcelona,
Spain

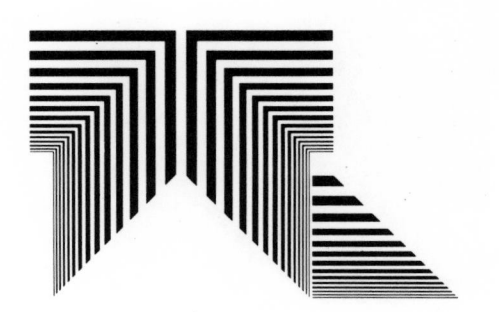

7/32
French Associates
(Translation agency)
Designer/Stuart Ash, Gottschalk & Ash
Limited, Toronto, Canada

7/33
Tecnicas Comunicacion
Designer/Francesc Guitart, Barcelona,
Spain

7/34
Bauplan
(Architectural promotion)
Designer/Michael Burke, London

7/35
Amilcare Pizzi
(Typographer)
Designer/Giulio Confalonieri, Milan, Italy

7/36
Sun Life Assurance Company of Canada (US)
(Life insurance company)
Designer/John German, Montreal, Canada

7/37
Dr Guylaine Lanctôt
(Medical clinic)
Designer/Jacque Roy, Quebec, Canada

7/38
Joe Dent
(Furniture removers and storers)
Designer/Jonathan De Morgan
Leeds, England

7/39
Meadway Radio Cars Ltd
(Taxi and car hire)
Designer/Collis Clements, Kent, England

8/1
VEB Messeprojekt Leipzig
(Exhibition contractors)
Designer/Horst Wendt, Berlin, DDR

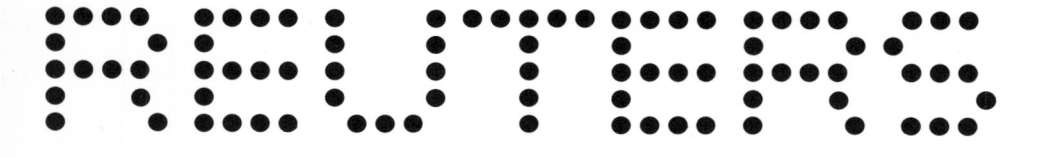

8/2
Reuters
(International news agency)
Designer/Alan Fletcher, Pentagram, London

Logotype derived from the punched tape
used by Reuters for transmitting
information

8/3
**The New Brunswick Telephone
Company Ltd**
Designer/Ernst Roch, Roch Design
Montreal, Canada

8/4
Copp Clark Ltd
(Publisher)
Designer/Stuart Ash, Gottschalk & Ash,
Toronto, Canada

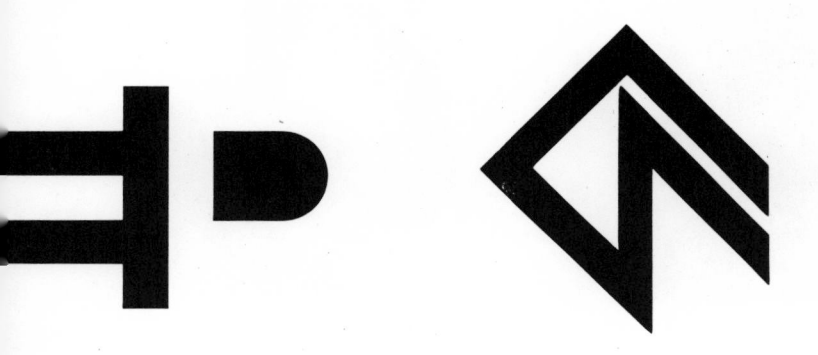

/5
es Éditions Particulières
(Publishers' mark)
Designer/Raudi Gandreau, Quebec,
Canada

/6
Komitee für Druck, Sofia
Designer/Stephen Kantscheff, Sofia,
Bulgaria

8/7
Oliver & Boyd
(Publisher)
Designer/not known

Mark for a series of science paperbacks

8/8
Behr
(Publisher)
Designer/Anton Stankowski, Stuttgart,
West Germany

8/9
Allen Lithographic
(Printers, stationers)
Designer/Albert Brebner, Edinburgh,
Scotland

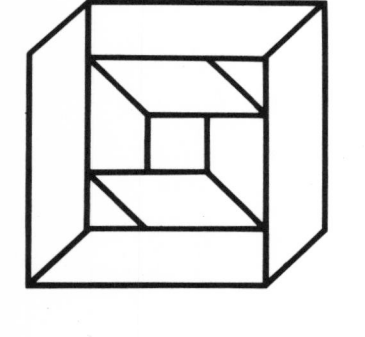

8/10
Essedi Editrice
(Publisher)
Designer/Giancarlo Iliprandi, Milan, Italy

8/11
Forum World Features
Designer/Banks and Miles, London

Original colours: black and blue

8/12
Mouton Publishing Company
(Publisher specialising in the field of the humanities)
Designer/Peter Brattinga, Amsterdam, Holland

8/13
Bell Canada
(Telephone and communications)
Designer/Burton Kramer, Burton Kramer Associates Limited, Toronto, Canada

8/14
Secter Films
(Film producers)
Designer/Robert Burns, Toronto, Canada

8/15
Cambridge University Press
(Publisher)
Designer/David Gentleman, London

Mark for a scientific series 'International Biological Programme'

8/16
Komitee für Fernsehen und Radio, Sofia
Designer/Stephen Kantscheff, Sofiå, Bulgaria

8/17
Canadian Broadcasting Corporation
Designer/Burton Kramer, Burton Kramer Associates Limited, Toronto, Canada.

Mark for the national as well as international Canadian radio and television system

8/18
The Chum Group
(Consortium of broadcasting companies)
Designer/Robert Burns, Toronto, Canada

8/19
Hoffmann-La Roche
Designer/Rolf Harder,
Montreal, Canada

Logotype for a magazine dealing with
aspects of anxiety

8/20
Penguin-Longman Books
(Publisher)
Designer/Hans Schleger and Associates,
London

8/21
New Left Books
(Publisher)
Designer/Ken Garland and Associates,
London

8/22
Alphabet Ltd
(Photosetter and silkscreen printer)
Designer/Darrell Ireland, Delaney and
Ireland, London

8/23
Spectrum Publishers
Designer/Wim Crouwel, TD Associatie voor
Total Design bv, Amsterdam, Holland

9/1
National Theatre (project)
Designer/Jean Robert,
Pentagram, London

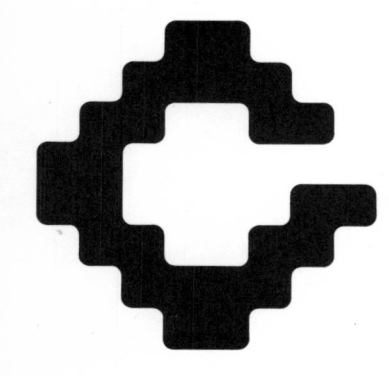 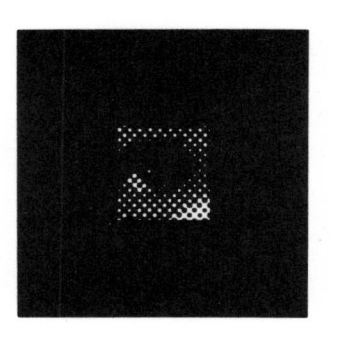 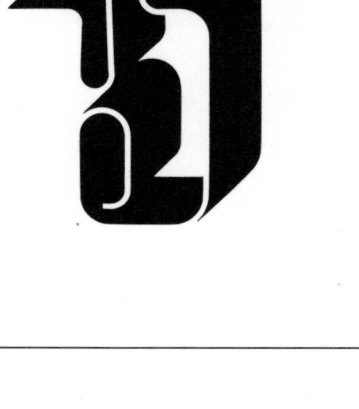

9/2
CISKA
(Theatre ticket office)
Designer/Ben Bos, TD Associatie voor Total
Design bv, Amsterdam, Holland

9/3
Speakeasy
(Discotheque)
Designer/Alan Fletcher, Pentagram, London

9/4
The Cinema of Amateur Films
Designer/Roman Rosyk, Wroclaw, Poland

9/5
London Film Production Fair
Designer/Kenneth Hollick FSIAD, London

9/6
Nepentha
(Night club)
Designer/Guilio Confalonieri, Milan, Italy

9/7
Saratoga Performing Arts Center
Designer/Robert P. Gersin, New York

9/8
Toronto Arts Foundation
(Theatrical Productions)
Designer/Stuart Ash, Gottschalk & Ash,
Toronto, Canada

9/9
Phonogram Limited
Designer/Linda Nicol

Mark for Vertigo records

9/10
**Music festival on the Black Sea Coast –
Stadt Burgas**
Designer/Stephan Kantscheff, Sofia,
Bulgaria

9/11
Arapahoe Chamber Orchestra
(Arapahoe is the name of a Colorado Indian
tribe)
Designer/Fred Colcer, Colorado, USA

9/12
State Operetta Theatre
Designer/Stephan Kantscheff, Sofia,
Bulgaria

9/13
Society for Modern Music
(Organisation promoting jazz and modern
music)
Designer/Fred Colcer, Colorado, USA

9/14
Eolina
(Music quartet)
Designer/Stephan Kantscheff, Sofia,
Bulgaria

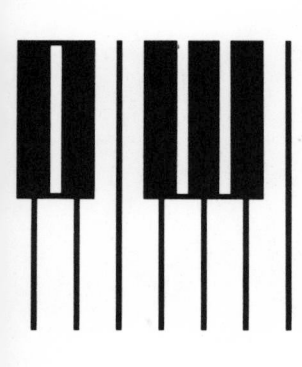

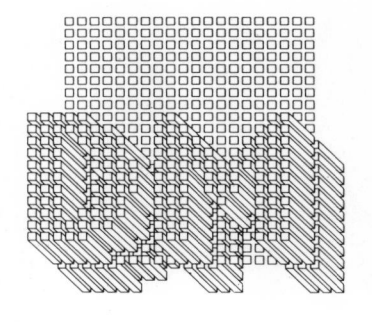

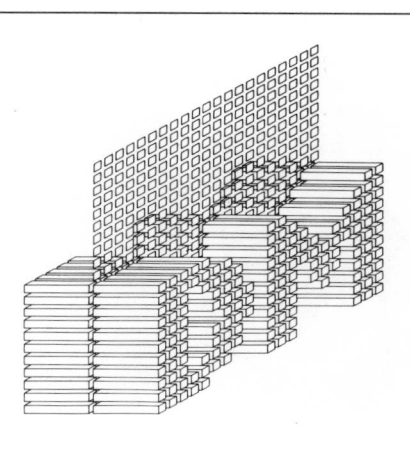

9/15
Olga Schewkenowa
(Mark for a pianist)
Designer/Stephan Kantscheff, Sofia,
Bulgaria

9/16
Choir Festival
Designer/Rosmarie Tissi, Atelier Odermatt
Tissi, Zurich, Switzerland

9/17
DM Gallery
(Art gallery)
Designer/David Brennan, London

Two of a set of linear designs

9/18
Inder
(Chess contest)
Designer/Félix Beltrán, Havana, Cuba

9/19
Sweatshop
(Sports equipment)
Designer/George Daulby, London

9/20
Olympic Games, Munich
Designer/Otl Aicher, West Germany

9/21
Nippon Bowl
(Bowling centre, Osaka, Japan)
Designer/Ivor Kaplin, Osaka, Japan

9/22
Le Comité Organisateur des Jeux Olympiques de 1976
(Olympic Games, Montreal)
Designer/Georges Huel, Georges Huel &
Associates Inc. Montreal, Canada

9/23
Canadian Hockey Industries Inc.
(Hockey and ski manufacturers)
Designer/Georges Huel, Georges Huel &
Associates Inc. Montreal, Canada

9/24
Kingston Racing Motors
(Manufacturers of racing motor cycles)
Designer/Keith Murgatroyd, Royle-
Murgatroyd Design Associates Limited,
London

9/25
British Gliding Association
(National gliding organisation)
Designer/Peter Wildbur, London

9/26
Club de Hockey National de Laval
(Hockey club)
Designer/Georges Huel, Montreal, Canada

9/27
Nautech
(Manufacturers of advanced yacht
equipment)
Designer/Terry Jeavons, Chichester, UK

9/28
Trissl Lift
(Ski lifts)
Designer/Anton Stankowski, Stuttgart,
West Germany

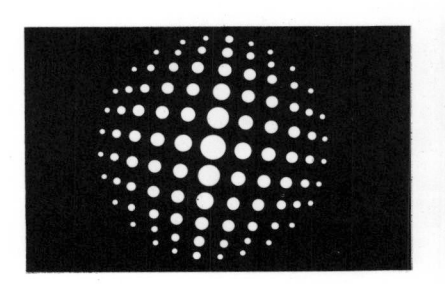

9/29
Nautitec Inc.
(Boat manufacturer)
Designer/Louis-André Rivard, Montreal,
Canada

9/30
Kitsilano Sailing School & Boat Rentals
Designer/Michael Pacey, Vancouver,
Canada

9/31
Gowen (Sails) Limited
(Sailmaker)
Designer/Negus & Negus, London

A mark to be used for printed matter and on
the clew of a sail, the traditional place for a
sailmaker's mark. In the latter case it would
be sewn or stencilled

9/32
Eurogolf
(Golfing organisation)
Designer/Ivor Kamlish FSIAD &
Associates, London

10/1
Dronten
(New town)
Designer/Ben Bos, TD Associatie voor Total
Design bv, Amsterdam, Holland

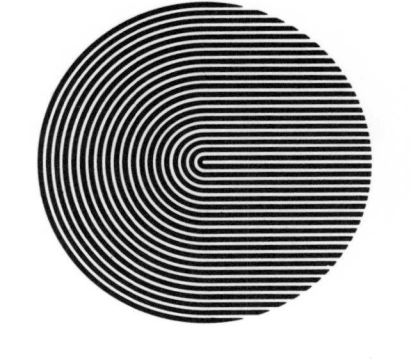

10/2
Convegno Quadri Provinciali del Pri
(Political emblem)
Designer/Michele Spera, Rome, Italy

10/3
League of Women Voters of
Massachusetts
Designer/Joe Selame, Selame Design,
Massachusetts, USA

The mark is composed of one geometric
element comprising the initials L,W,V

10/4
Simposio de Criminalistica
Designers/Félix Beltrán and Dagoberto
Marcelo, Havana, Cuba

10/5
Canadian Save the Children Fund
(Canadian branch of an international welfare
and development agency for underprivileged
youth)
Designer/Robert Burns, Toronto, Canada

10/6
Bolton Metropolitan Borough
(Civic Authority)
Designer/Kenneth Adshead FSIAD

An heraldic pun combining an arrow (bolt) with a crown or Anglo-Saxon palisade (tun)

10/7
Innenministerium der BRD
(Competition for environmental protection symbol for Ministry of the Interior of the Federal German Republic)
Designer/Anton Stankowski, Stuttgart, West Germany

10/8
Canadian Association for Retarded Children
Designer/Rolf Harder,
Montreal, Canada

10/9
Scottish National Party
Designer/Julien Gibb, Glasgow, Scotland

Mark based on St Andrew's cross and thistle, Scotland's national flower

10/10
Littercheck
(Public information campaign)
Designer/Glen Arnold, Stewart & Morrison Limited, Toronto, Canada

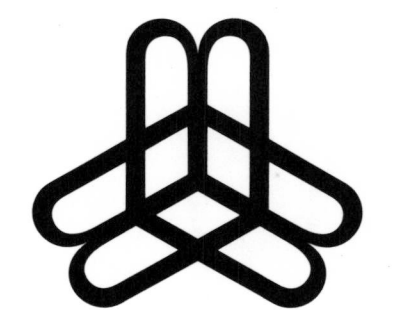

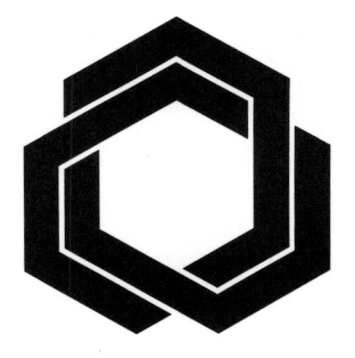

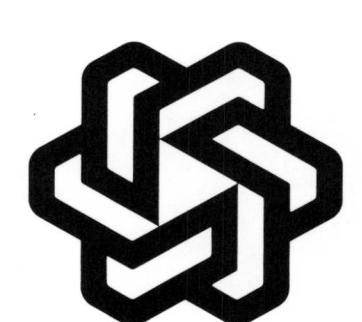

10/11
Area Museums Service for South East England
Designer / Richard Daynes FSIAD, London

Mark based on salomonic knot motif from Tunisia

10/12
Scottish Arts Council
Designer / Albert Brebner, Edinburgh, Scotland

10/13
National Arts Centre
(Centre for the cultivation of the performing arts)
Designer / Ernst Roch, Roch Design, Montreal, Canada

The symbol is based on the hexagonal plans of the three architectural structures of the complex

10/14
McCord Museum
Designer / Fritz Gottschalk, Gottschalk & Ash Toronto, Canada

10/15
Canadian Craft Council
(National organisation of craftsmen)
Designers / Tim Nielsen and Burton Kramer, Burton Kramer Associates Limited, Toronto Canada

10/16
West Midland Arts
(Regional co-ordinating arts association)
Designer/Keith Murgatroyd, Royle
Murgatroyd Design, London

10/17
Leeds Polytechnic
(A polytechnic comprising four colleges of
further education)
Designers/ THB Russell MSIAD and
PS Walker

A mark with variation below which reflects
the interdisciplinary collaboration and
relationships of four major colleges (see also
page 32)

10/18
University of Massachusetts Press
Designers/David Lock and Diana Smith,
Lock Pettersen Limited, London

Design based on an early press mark in the
form of a tree

10/19
**Ontario Educational Communications
Authority**
(Provincial government education television,
radio and publishing)
Designer/Burton Kramer, Burton Kramer
Associates Limited, Toronto, Canada

Design basis: Multiple, revolving letter 'O'
for Ontario Broadcasting.

10/20
**Conseil Supérieur de la Création
Esthétique Industrielle**
(National council of industrial design)
Designer/Jean Widmer, Paris, France

10/21
Metric Commission (Government)
(Metric conversion in Canada)
Designer/Stuart Ash, Gottschalk & Ash,
Toronto, Canada

10/22
Partito Repubblicano
(Italian political party)
Designer/Michele Spera, Rome, Italy

Original colours: red and green

0/23
Kunst & Bedrÿf
(Foundation for art and industry)
Designer/Ben Bos, TD Associate voor Total
Design bv, Amsterdam, Holland

0/24
**Sonja Henie-Neils Onstad Foundations,
Oslo**
(Museum and cultural centre)
Designer/Rosmarie Tissi, Atelier Odermatt
& Tissi, Zurich, Switzerland

Mark based on a stylised flame. A rather
unusual example of application is the reproduction of the emblem in a floral display
about 7m in diameter in the courtyard of the
Museum

10/25
**Seventh World Congress of Sociology–
Varna, Black Sea**
Designer/Stephan Kantscheff, Sofia,
Bulgaria

10/26
The University of Aston in Birmingham
Designer/Keith Murgatroyd, Royle
Murgatroyd Design Associates, London

10/27
Salisbury & Wells Theological College
Designer/Keith Murgatroyd, Royle
Murgatroyd Design Associates, London

10/28
Comité Européen Fabricants de Sucre
(World marketing of sugar)
Designer/Roger Simmons NDD, MSIAD,
Bath, UK

Prize-winning design for a universal mark
symbolising sugar

10/29
**Vitreous Enamel Development
Council Ltd**
Designer/John Pearce, Colchester, UK

10/30
Pharma Information
(Press and public relations)
Designer/George Staehelin, Pentagram,
Zurich, Switzerland

Mark of the central information office of the
research-based pharmaceutical companies
Ciba-Geigy — Hoffmann — La Roche and
Sandoz

10/31
Conseil de sécurité publique
Communauté urbaine de Montréal
(Police force)
Designer/Robert Monette, Montréal,
Canada

10/32
Centre de Création Industrielle
(Design centre)
Designer/Jean Widmer, Paris, France

10/33
Habitat, the United Nations Conference
on Human Settlements
Designer/Graham Hughes, Vancouver,
Canada

The mark has not been made copyright
as a matter of policy

10/34
Islamic Solidarity
Designer/Alan Fletcher, Pentagram, London

The mark combines six crescents
representing the six Islamic countries.
Colours: black, white and green

10/35
Office for the promotion of trade with
China
Designer/Wolfgang Heuwinkel, Bergisch
Gladback, West Germany

10/36
La Kateri
(Persian and Himalayan cats)
Designer/Ginette La Berge, Quebec,
Canada

10/37
Metro Zoo
(Zoological society and zoo)
Designer/Peter Ulmer, Stewart & Morrison
Limited, Toronto, Canada

10/38
**Mark for a Bulgarian exhibition of
Oceanography in Okinawa, Japan**
Designer/Stephen Kantscheff, Sofia,
Bulgaria

10/39
Student Advisory Council (Orpington)
Designer/Michael Burke, London

Registering a trademark

The trademark designer should have a working knowledge of the law in relation to the copyright protection which it offers, and the types of mark which can be registered.

Not all clients wish to protect their marks from infringement by imitation or mis-representation but a successful mark which has been registered will have a considerable asset value and this has been enhanced since the 1938 Act which gave statutory approval to the assignment of a registered trademark enabling a mark to be traded as an independent piece of property. In some cases a requirement to register a design may influence aspects of the design itself.

Registration of a mark at the Patent Office only gives protection in this country (at the time of writing) and registration in other countries requires application in each of the countries concerned. It is likely that simultaneous registration for other European countries will be available in the near future if the draft proposals for a proposed European trademark are implemented (see book list).

In the UK it is possible to register a mark at Stationers' Hall for the purpose of recording and supplying proof of the existence of a mark on a given date.

Stationers' Hall is not a government department and registration provides no protection of the mark in the case of infringement but it does provide evidence of the existence of the mark which may be required if full Patent Office registration is sought at a later stage. Registration is retained for seven years unless renewal is requested.

The Trademark Acts

The Trade Mark Registration Act was first passed in 1875 and the current Act in 1938. This act governs the registration of trade-marks in this country with the exception of two specialised forms of marks each of which, for historical reasons, has its own Registry. These are for marks for cotton goods at the Manchester Branch and for metal goods at the Cutlers' Company in Sheffield.

Registering a trademark

The following notes are only intended as a general guide to the law in this country and for more detailed information the reader should obtain the current version of *Applying for a Trade Mark,* published by HMSO.

The diagram below shows the stages in the registration of a trademark. At the present time trademarks are only accepted for registration in relation to goods and not to services, so that it is not possible to register a trademark for, say banking, travel services or

Stages in the registration of a trademark	1 Application received	2 Application examined	3 Results of examination conveyed to applicant
	Mark added to search list of pending applications	Formal requirements checked. Specification of goods edited; allocated to class. Search made for conflicting marks. Examined for distinctiveness and deception.	Objections raised. Oral hearing (or written sub-mission). *Application accepted,* possibly subject to conditions or amendment, or *Application refused* (subject to appeal)

professional services. The Mathys Committee in a report published in 1974 recommended that the Trade Mark Act should be extended to cover marks used for services so it may not be too long before protection is available for a wide range of services.

One of the requirements for registration is that the mark must be distinctive. Since the mark can be in the form of a word and/or an image then one or other of these elements must be distinctive in itself. In general terms this means that words or images of a common nature in general use in connection with the product cannot be registered. Invented words can be used providing that they are not merely phonetic variation of words in general use. Invented words which are similar to other registered words such as Alka-Vescent and Alka-Seltzer or Motricine and Motorine would not be accepted.

To achieve distinctiveness is not particularly difficult and very often only a small amendment is necessary to clear this obstacle. Sometimes the mark will be accepted on the basis of distinctiveness if the class of goods claimed is limited, but some marks are distinctive in relation to some goods but not in relation to others.

A second important requirement is that the mark must not be deceptive either in the sense of implying characteristics which the

TRADE MARKS JOURNAL.

LIST OF APPLICATIONS

FOR

THE REGISTRATION OF TRADE MARKS

Under the Trade Marks Registration Act, 1875.

No. 1.] WEDNESDAY, MAY 3, 1876. [*Price One Shilling.*

Trade Mark.	Name, Address, and Calling of Applicant.	Class of Goods.	Description of Goods.	Number given by Registrar.	Date of Application received.	If Mark used prior to 13th August 1875, how long used.
TRADE MARK. DR. LOCOCK	CHARLES GEORGE JOHNSON DA SILVA, 26, Bride Lane, London; Merchant and Manufacturer.	1	Acids, Alkalies, and Dyes.	93	3rd Jan. 1876.	Thirty-six years before 3rd Jan. 1876.
AMIES PATENT CHEMICAL NEW MANURE	WILLIAM SMITH AMIES, 284, Liverpool Road, Islington, London; Manufacturer.	2	A Chemical Substance used as an Artificial Manure for Agricultural and Horticultural Purposes.	60	1st Jan. 1876.	Two years before 31st Dec. 1875.
TRADE MARK. DR. LOCOCK	CHARLES GEORGE JOHNSON DA SILVA, 26, Bride Lane, London; Merchant and Manufacturer.	3	Tinctures, Extracts, Barks, Patent Medicines, and Cod Liver Oil.	93	3rd Jan. 1876.	Thirty-six years before 3rd Jan. 1876.

Front cover of the first Trade Marks Journal, 1876

Application accepted	5 Advertised in the Trade Marks Journal	6 Unopposed	7 Application registered
	Opposed. Oral hearing.		
	Application accepted, possibly subject to conditions or application refused (subject to appeal)		

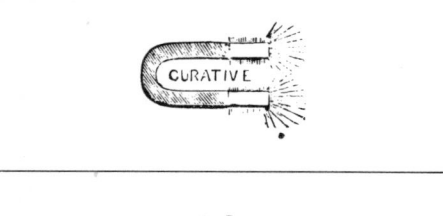

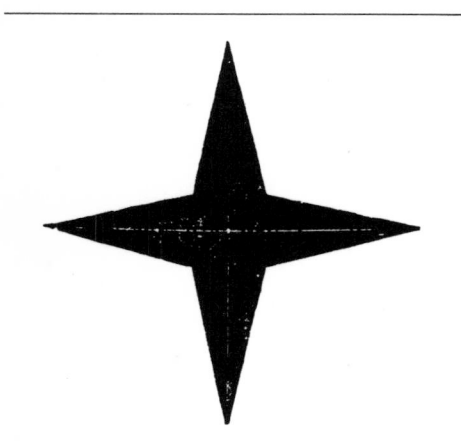

(above and opposite)
Trademarks appearing in the first Trade
Marks Journal, 1876

product does not possess or in closely
resembling an existing mark for the same or
similar goods: For example, an image of a
shell would stand little chance of being
accepted for a petroleum product but would
probably be acceptable for many other
classes of goods. The classification of goods
for registration is split up into 34 classes and
is set out in the publication already
mentioned, *Applying for a Trade Mark.*

In addition to the above requirements there
are some words and images which are not
acceptable and these include the Royal arms
and crests, national flags and devices
relating to the armed services.

If the trademark design successfully passes
these criteria then it is published in the *Trade
Marks Journal* and a month is allowed during
which period any person may lodge object-
ions to the proposed mark.

If there is no opposition the mark is registered and lasts for a period of seven years.
After seven years the mark may be renewed
for periods of fourteen years at a time.

The designer or sponser of a mark can make
a search at the Trade Marks Branch of the
Patent Office before application to ensure
that the proposed mark is not similar to any
existing marks and this would reduce the risk
of having an application turned down or
delays in having to modify a design.

Another category of mark which can be
registered is the Certification trade mark.
These are marks intended to certify that the
goods to which they are applied comply with
certain characteristics whether of origin,
material, method of manufacture, quality or
accuracy. The applicant must not trade in
these goods himself but may license others
to manufacture and market them. Well
known examples of such marks are the wool
mark of the International Wool Secretariat,
the 'kite' device of the British Standards
Institution and the 'orb and cross' device of
the Harris Tweed Association.

Professional advice is available about all
aspects of trademark registration from
members of the Institute of Trade Mark
Agents. The trademark agent's role is to
research new trademarks at home and
abroad, to deal with the procedural details
of registration and to negotiate in any
disputes concerning trademarks. His help is
particularly valuable in sorting out the
various national requirements for European
or overseas registration.

Trade Mark.	Name, Address, and Calling of Applicant.	Class of Goods.	Description of Goods.	Number given by Registrar.	Date of Application received.	If Mark used prior to 13th August 1875, how long used.

No. 1.

No. 2.

No. 3.

No. 914.

	Name, Address, and Calling of Applicant.	Class of Goods.	Description of Goods.	Number given by Registrar.	Date of Application received.	If Mark used prior to 13th August 1875, how long used.
No. 1.	MICHAEL ARTHUR BASS, on behalf of BASS AND CO., Burton-on-Trent, Brewers.	43	Pale Ale.	1	1st Jan. 1876.	Twenty years before 31st Dec. 1875.
No. 2.	MICHAEL ARTHUR BASS, on behalf of BASS AND CO., Burton-on-Trent, Brewers.	43	Burton Ales.	2	1st Jan. 1876.	Eighteen years before 31st Dec. 1875.
No. 3.	MICHAEL ARTHUR BASS, on behalf of BASS AND CO., Burton-on-Trent, Brewers.	43	[Brown Beers and Stouts.	3	1st Jan. 1876.	Eleven years before 31st Dec. 1875.
No. 914.	MICHAEL ARTHUR BASS, on behalf of BASS AND CO., Burton-on-Trent, Brewers.	43	Pale Ale.	914	17th Jan. 1876.	Twenty years before 15th Jan. 1876.

Book list

Form and Communication, Walter Diethelm, Editions ABC, Zurich, Switzerland, 1974

Top symbols & trademarks of the world (7 volumes), edited by Franco Maria Ricci and Corinna Ferrari, Deco Press, Milan, Italy, 1974

Signs and symbols in graphic communication; Design Quarterly no. 62, 1965, Walker Art Center, USA

Symbols sourcebook, an authoritive guide to International graphic symbols, Henry Dreyfus, McGraw-Hill Book Company, New York, USA, 1972

Glyphs (newsletters) published at intervals by Glyphs, Inc. an organisation for the development of universal graphic symbols. Kent, Ct 06757, USA

A century of trademarks (A commentary on the work and history of the Trade Marks Registry) The Patent Office, Department of Trade, HMSO, London, 1976

Proposed European trademark (Preliminary draft), Department of Trade and Industry, HMSO, London, 1973

Trademarks, Peter Wildbur, Studio Vista, London and Reinhold Publishing Corporation, New York, 1966

Organisations

The Patent Office
25 Southampton Buildings, London WC2A 1AY.

The Manchester Branch,
Trade Marks Registry
Baskerville House, Browncross Street, New Bailey Street, Salford, M3 5FU.

Cutler's Hall, Church Street,
Sheffield S1 1HG.

Stationers' Hall Registry
Stationers Hall Court, London EC4.

The Institute of Trade Mark Agents
69 Cannon Street, London EC4N 5AB.

Index of designers
(Single numerals refer to numbered
trademarks between pages 10–32. Numerals
separated by an oblique refer to section
number followed by trademark number
between pages 49–122).

Adam, Peter 3/1, 6/13
Adshead, Kenneth 10/6
Aicher, Otl 15, 36, 38, 9/20
Arnold, Glen 2/10, 6/6, 10/10
Ash, Stuart 2/7, 2/28, 3/11, 3/13, 4/23, 5/7, 5/25, 6/7, 6/9, 7/30, 7/32, 8/4, 9/8, 10/21
Atelier Stankowski & Partner 1/10, 3/4, 4/1, 6/4

Banks and Miles 2/14, 4/13, 8/11
Bass, Saul & Associates 3/7
Bellemare, Raymond 2/9, 3/18, 5/5, 5/22, 7/16, 7/22
Beltrán, Félix 4/14, 4/28, 6/12, 7/28, 9/18, 10/4
Bernardini, Walter 5/14
Bing-Wah, Hon 4/16
Bos, Ben 2/22, 5/12, 7/23, 9/2, 10/1, 10/23
Brattinga, Pieter 8/12
Braunstein & McLaren Associates 37
Brebner, Albert 2/15, 5/15, 5/24, 7/15, 7/19, 8/9, 10/12
Brennan, David 9/17
Burke, Michael 7/34, 10/39
Burns, Robert 5/21, 7/6, 8/14, 8/18, 10/5
Butts, Mike 7/12

Chwast, Seymour 2
Clements, Collis 4/18, 7/39
Colcer, Fred 9/11, 9/13
Confalonieri, Giulio 7/35, 9/6
Cook and Shanosky Associates Inc. 16
Coubertin, Pierre de 9
Crouwel, Wim 7/8, 8/23

Cutini, Rinaldo 5/10, 6/10, 6/14, 6/24, 7/21, 7/26

Daulby, George 4/5, 9/19
Daynes, Richard 14, 6/21, 10/11
Dodd, Ivan and Robin 5/29
Dutton, Norbert 3

Eurographic Ltd 3/20

Flemming, Allan 1
Fletcher, Alan 31, 1/5, 4/8, 6/19, 7/29, 8/2, 9/3, 10/34
Forbes, Colin 4/8, 4/15, 9/1
Ford, Ron 24
Fraser, June 7/12
Frutiger, Adrian 3/10

Gagnon, Valkus Inc. 6
Gandreau, Raudi 8/5
Garland, Ken and Associates 5/17, 8/21
Gauld, Peter 29, 4/27
Gentleman, David 32, 35, 1/14, 7/3, 8/15
German, John 7/36
Gersin, Robert 2/19, 4/17, 9/7
Gerstner, Gredinger + Kutter 12
Gibb, Julian 10/9
Glaser, Milton 2
Gottschalk, Fritz 5/25
Graff, Carl B 27
Guitart, Francesc 2/1, 2/25, 5/26, 7/31, 7/33

Hablutzel, Peter 2/8
Harder, Rolf 5/2, 5/8, 8/19, 10/8
Harper, Irving 8

Harrison, John 3/19, 4/2, 4/4
Hauser Associates 7/25
Heuwinkel, Wolfgang 2/12, 2/17, 4/19, 10/35
Hewat/Swift/Walters 7/4
Hoffman, Jürgen 6/23, 7/18
Hollender, Jan 4/24
Hollick Kenneth 4, 9/5
Huel, Georges 34, 3/14, 9/22, 9/23, 9/26
Hughes, Graham 10/33

Illiprandi, Giancarlo 6/15, 8/10
Ireland, Darrell 8/22

Jacob, Ronald 2/23
Jaggie, Fredy 5/25
Jasinski, Jaroslaw 4/30, 5/3, 5/20, 5/30
Jeavons, Terry 9/27
Joksch, Gerhard 36
Justason, Alistair 2/2

Kamlish, Ivor and Associates 9/32
Kantscheff, Stephan 3/22, 5/4, 5/6, 5/23,
8/6, 8/16, 9/10, 9/12, 9/14, 9/15, 10/25,
10/38
Kaplin, Ivor 9/21
Kern, Alfred 36
Kinneir Calvert Tuhill 2/13
Kleefeld, Hans 1/13, 2/5, 3/9
Kramer, Burton 30, 4/12, 7/5, 8/13, 8/17,
10/15, 10/19
Kräuchi, Peter 5, 20

La Berge, Ginette 10/36
L'Allier, Denis 5/18
Lanari, Roberto 1/9

Landor Associates 4/26, 7/2
Le Brocquy, Louis 22, 25
Lenz, Eugen and Max 13
Lippincott & Margulies 1/12, 4/3, 4/11
Lock, David 2/3, 3/21, 5/13, 10/18

Magalhâes, Aloisio 1/2, 3/9, 7/7, 7/10
Marber, Romek 17, 18
Massey, John 23
Monette, Robert 10/31
Morgan, Jonathan de 29, 7/24, 7/38
Murgatroyd, Keith 2/24, 9/24, 10/16, 10/26,
10/27

Negus & Negus 3/5, 6/2, 9/31
Nemitz, Dieter 4/20
Nielson, Tim 10/15

Odermatt, Siegfried 4/22, 6/11

Pacey, Michael 1/7, 1/8, 6/20, 7/20, 9/30
Pearce, John 10/29
Pettersen, Tor 1/1, 4/7, 4/10, 5/1, 5/13, 5/28
Prüget, Herbert 5/16

Randak, Charles 3/8
Redig, Joaquim 1/3, 2/11, 2/16, 2/27
Reifenstahl, Peter 6/3
Rivard, Louis-André 7/14, 9/29
Robert, Jean 4/15, 9/1
Roch, Ernst 1/11, 6/1, 8/3, 10/13
Rodrigues, Rafael 1/3
Rosyk, Roman 5/19, 9/4
Rousset, Brigitte 3/12
Roy, Jacque 7/37

Russell, THB 40, 10/17

Saroglia, Francesco 21
Schleger, Hans and Associates 8/20
Schrofer, Jurriaan 5/11
Scott, Patrick 11
Selame, Joe 1/6, 5/27, 6/17, 10/3
Simard, Claude A 4/29, 7/27
Simmons, Roger 1/4, 4/9, 10/28
Smith, Diana 10/18
Smith, Stephen 3/19
Spera, Michele 7/11, 10/2, 10/22
Staehelin, George 10/30
Stankowski, Anton 7, 1/10, 2/6, 3/4, 4/1, 6/4, 7/13, 8/8, 9/28, 10/7
Stegmeijer, John 7/1
Steiner, Henry 3/2, 3/6, 4/31, 7/9

Thumb Design Partnership 2/18
Tissi, Rosmarie 4/21, 5/9, 6/5, 6/16, 9/16, 10/24
Tucker, Michael 4/6
Tutssel, Glen 6/8

Ulmer, Peter 10/37

Vail, Ken 6/22
Vasarely, Victor 3/17

Waddell, Malcolm 2/4
Walker, P S 10/17
Ward, Peter 2/26
Waterfield, Derek J 2/21
Weerd, Wim van der 2/20, 6/18
Wendt, Horst 8/1

Widmer, Jean 4/25, 10/20, 10/32
Wildbur, Peter 19, 7/17, 9/25
Wilson, Norman 3/3

Yaneff, Chris 26
Yoshiska, Kenichi 10

Index of clients
(Single numerals refer to numbered trademarks between pages 10–32. Numerals separated by an oblique refer to section number followed by trademark number between pages 49–122).

Aberdeen Harbour Board 2/15
Abitibi Provincial Paper 5/21
Aeroport de Paris 3/10
Alarma 5/12
Alireza Group of Companies 1/1
Allen Lithographic 8/9
Alphabet Ltd 8/22
Applied Research and Management Company 7/14
Apotheke Sammet 6/11
Arapahoe Chamber Orchestra 9/11
Area Museums Service for South East England 10/11
Arflex 6/15
Artone 2
Associated Adhesives Ltd 29

Backerei Burkhardt Volketswil 6/16
Banco Mercantil de Pernambuco 7/7
Barnards Wire Fencing 18
Bauplan 7/34
Behr 8/8
Bell Canada 8/13
Bellemare, Raymond 7/22
Bennett Ltd, Reginald 4/23
Benz AG 4/21
Ber Gold Inc. 6/7
Biode Pharmaceutical Industries Ltd 5/28
Bloom & Son Incorporated, William 2/23
Bolton, B T 7/24
Bolton Metropolitan Borough 10/6
British Airways 3/5
British Gliding Association 9/25
British Industrial Holdings Ltd 4/4
British Steel Corporation 32, 1/14

Bulgarische Staatseisenbahnen 3/22
Büro für Werbung, Organisation und Sozialprobleme 13
bv Bouwbedrijf Hazenberg 2/20

Cambridge University Press 8/15
Canada Systems Group 7/5
Canadian Association for Retarded Children 10/8
Canadian Broadcasting Corporation 8/17
Canadian Craft Council 10/15
Canadian Hockey Industries Inc. 9/35
Canadian National Railways 1
Canadian Save the Children Fund 10/15
Canadian Sociology and Anthropology Association 30
Cape Boards & Panels Ltd 4/15
Castagna Arredamenti 5/10
Casu, Bonaria 7/21
Central Office of Information Training Services Agency 7/12
Central Sewing Machine Inc. 5/18
Centre de Création Industrielle 10/32
Certina 27
Champlain Container Corporation 5/7
Chelsea Drug & Chemical Company 5/1
Chicago Pharmacal 23
Chrysler Internation 3/15
Chum Group, The 8/18
Cinema of Amateur Films, The 9/4
CISKA 9/2
Citroën 3/16
Claude Neon Industries Ltd 5/25
Cliche-Schwitter AG 12
Club de Hockey National de Laval 9/26

Colonia Provision Co Inc. 6/17
Comité European Fabricants de Sucre 10/28
Comité Organisateur des Jeux Olympiques de
1976, Le 34, 9/22
Compagnie Financière et du Crédit SA 35, 7/3
CompAir Ltd 4/6
Commission de Transport de La Ville de Laval,
La, 3/14
Communikart Inc. 7/27
Conseil Supérieur de la Création Esthetique
Industrielle 10/20
Conseil de Sécurité Publique Communauté
Urbaine de Montréal 10/31
Consolidated Foods Inc. 4/26
Construtora Queiroz Galvao 2/11
Convegno Quadri Provinciali del Pri 10/2
Co-operative of Disabled Workmen in Stupsk
5/3
Copp Clark Ltd 8/4
Crosby Books 6/2
Cunic Partition Systems 17
Cyrmac Plastics Inc. 5/22

Darby, John G 28
De Gruyter 6/18
Delanair Ltd 4/10
Delta Acceptance Corporation Ltd 26
Dent, Joe 7/38
Deschamps Excavation Inc. 2/9
Designs, CI, Inc. 7/25
Design, DI, & Development Consultants 7/30
Deutsches Fernschen 7
D M Gallery 9/17
Docenave, Vale do Rio Doce Navegacão 3/9
Dronten 10/1

Éditions Particulières, Les 8/5
Elton, K 4/24
English Property Corporation Ltd 2/26
Eolina 9/14
Equal Opportunities Commission 4
Erco Leuchten GmbH 36
Essedi Editrice 8/10
Essilor 4/25
Eurogolf 9/32

FBG-Trident 4/13
Flughafen 3/4
Forum World Features 8/11
Four C's Aviaries Ltd, The 6/8
Francine Vandeluc Tricot 5/5
French Associates 7/32
Friesland Bank 7/8
Funfstrahl 5/6
Furnas Centrais Elétricas 1/3

Gebrüder Heinemann 6/19
Gebr. Van Heeswyk 2/22
Gemeinnützige Siedlungsgellschaft
Gronauer Wald 2/17
Glen Abbey Community 2/4
Gowen (Sails) Ltd 9/31
Graells, Enric 7/31
Graff, A 6/3
Graphic Statement, The 7/20
Grupo Nacional 7/10
Grupo Paraiso 1/9
Guylaine Lanctôt, Dr, 7/37

Habitat, the United Nations Conference
on Human Settlements 10/33

Harris, Kenneth 24
Helix Investments 7/6

Henie-Neils Onstad Foundations, Sonja 10/24
Heyer Paper Ltd, John 4/19
Hoffmann-La Roche 8/19
Holroyd Construction Ltd 2/24
Hong Kong Air International Ltd 3/2, 3/6
Howard Machinery 4/3
Hull & Humber Cargo Handling Co Ltd 3/20

Imasco Ltd 5/2
Imobiliária Novo Mundo 2/27
Inder 9/18
Innenministerium der BRD 10/7
Interlabor SA 7/23
International Nickel Co of Canada Ltd, The 1/13
International Olympic Committee 9, 33
International Wool Secretariat 21
Irish Double Jersey Association 11
Irish Flock 4/5
Irish Silk Poplin 22
Islamic Solidarity 10/34
Isseks Brothers Inc. 2/19
Itaipu Binacional 1/2

Jardine Flemming & Co Ltd 7/9
Jednosc 5/30
Jobling Ltd, James A 4/11
Johnson & Nephew 4/2

Kateri, La 10/36
Kiekbusch, Dieter 5/16
Kilkenny Design Workshops 25
Kingston Racing Motors 9/24

Kitsilano Sailing School 9/30
Komitee fur Druck 8/6
Komitee fur Fernsehen und Radio 8/16
Kunst & Bedrÿf 10/23
Kuwait National Petroleum Company 1/5
Kytta 6/4

Lamper 5/26
Land Hessen 2/6
Lapidus, Luis 7/28
Law Society, The 14
League of Women Voters of Massachusetts
10/3
Lea Valley Regional Park Authority 2/3
Leeds Polytechnic 40, 10/17
Liberia Borghese 6/10
Littercheck 10/10
Living Aids Ltd 5/14
Loganair 3/8
London Film Production Fair 9/5
Lucas Industries 4/8

McCord Museum 10/14
Mackarl Electronics Inc. 4/31
McLair, Nicol Associates 7/19
Marathon Realty Co Ltd, Town Centre 2/2
Marcello Masi 6/24
Maritime Computers Ltd 7/18
Meadway Radio Cars Ltd 7/39
Mediceletrica 4/14
Mettler & Co Ltd 5/9
Metric Commission 10/21
Metropolitan Toronto & Region, Conservation
Authority 2/10
Metro Zoo 10/37

Miller Inc., Herman 8
Milton Laundry 6/22
Mouton Publishing Company 8/12
Music Festival on the Black Sea Coast 9/10
National Arts Centre 10/13
National Bus Company 3/3
National Theatre 9/1
National Water Council 2/14
National Westminster Bank Group 7/4
Nautech 9/27
Nautitic Inc. 9/29
Nepentha 9/6
New Brunswick Telephone Company Ltd,
The 8/3
New Gold Star Mines 1/8
New Left Books 8/21
Nippon Bowl 9/21
Norcount Realty Control Corporation 2/28
Nordet Inc., Le 7/16
Neuva Linea 2/25

Oakhurst Farms 1/11
Oakville Transit 3/13
Occulenti 7/1
Office for the promotion of trade with China
10/35
Oliver & Boyd 8/7
Olympic Games, Munich 15, 38, 9/20
Ontario Educational Communications
Authority 10/19
Ontario Trucking Association 3/1
Overseas Computer Consultants 7/17
Overseas Containers Ltd 3/19

Parsons & Sons Ltd, A J 4/9

Partito Republicano 10/22
Pausa Mössingen 4/1
Penguin-Longman Books 8/20
Pezos 5/20
Pharmacie Centre 6/1
Pharma information 10/30
Phonogram Ltd 9/9
Pizzi, Amilicare 7/35
Plessey Company Ltd, The 3
Points East 6/6
Polyzathe BV 5/11
Prückel, H 6/5

Quebec Hydro-Electric 6
Queenswear (Canada) Ltd 5/8
Quick Maid Rental Services Ltd 5/17

Reed Paper Ltd 4/12
Régie Nationale des Usines Renault 3/17
Reilly Lock Corporation 6/9
Resilience Ltd 19
Reunión Nacional de Investigación 4/28
Reuters 8/2
Rock Townsend 7/29
Rockwell International 3/7
Royer, Royer, Thivierge 4/29
Rug Tufters Inc. 6/13
Rutan Transport Inc. 3/18

Saint-en-Yvelines 2/13
Salisbury & Wells Theological College 10/27
Sandell Perkins Ltd 4/27
Saratoga Performing Arts Center Inc. 9/7
Scarborough Town Centre 2/5
Schelling Wellpappen AG 4/22

Schwihag GMBH 2/12
Scott Energy Systems 1/6
Scottish Arts Council 10/12
Scottish National Party 10/9
Secter Films 8/14
Selection Thomson Ltd 7/15
Servienge Companhia Serviços de Engenharia 2/16
Seventh World Congress of Sociology 10/25
Sheerness Steel 1/12
Shinko Electric Company Ltd 10
Sim Ltd, Tom 2/18
Simposio de Criminalistica 10/14
Site Oil Tools Ltd 1/7
Small Industries Council for Rural Areas of Scotland 5/24
Société des Autoroutes du Sud de la France 3/12
Société de Développement de la Baie James 2/8
Society for Modern Music 9/13
Soler Lavernia 2/1
Söll 1/10
Sound Investment 6/20
Spadaro Ventura SPA 6/14
Speakeasy 9/13
Spectrum Publishers 8/23
Stadtsparkasse Köln 7/13
State National Bank of El Paso 7/2
State Operetta Theatre 9/12
Statler Tissue Corporation 5/27
Stella-Meta Filters Ltd 4/7
Stewarts Supermarkets (Belfast) Ltd 6/21
Student Advisory Council (Orpington) 10/39
Sudbury Transit 3/11

Sun Life Assurance Company of Canada 7/36
Sweatshop 9/19
Swiss Gymnastic Association 5
SWIT 4/30

Tecnicas Comunicacion 7/33
Technitron Group, The 4/17
Tomeucci, Adolfo 7/26
Tonsos 5/23
Toronto Arts Foundation 9/8
Transtec International Freight Services Ltd 3/21
Travel bag factory 5/19
Trissl Lift 9/28

Ulster Carpets 5/29
Unilever International 4/18
United States Department of Transportation 16
University of Aston in Birmingham, The 10/26
University of Massachusetts Press 10/18
Urbana Insieme SRL 7/11
Ursula 6/12
Uspech 5/4

VEB Kalksandsteinwerk Elsterwerda 4/20
VEB Messeprojekt Leipzig 8/1
Vitreous Enamel Development Council 10/29

Wainwright & Co Ltd, John 1/4
Wallis Laboratories 5/13
Warrington & Sons Ltd, Thomas 2/21
West Midland Arts 10/16
Wilson (Twines) Ltd, John 5/15
Wilson Walton Signs Ltd 31

Wine Attic, The 6/23

York Centre 2/7
Yue Sang Engineering Ltd 4/16